Enneagram of Personality

A Beginners Guide To Self-Discovery for Psychological and Spiritual Growth Via The 9 Personality Types

LEANNE WALTERS

ENNEAGRAM OF PERSONALITY

CONTENTS

SPECIAL BONUS!

Want These 2 Bonus Books for <u>free</u>?

Get FREE, unlimited access to these and all of my new books by joining My Book Community!

Introduction

Dearest Reader,

Let me paint you a picture on the canvas...this time, with my keypad.

I'll tell you the story of a young girl. An adventurous, strong-willed, and unstable young girl named Leanne, who felt like a rebel. Leanne wanted a change of everything—her environment, her attitude, her family and friends, etc. At that time, she felt she was misunderstood and she started asking questions—"Who am I? Is there anything good coming in the future? What's the meaning of life or loyalty? Why does evil prevail more often than good?"

Trying to find answers to this barrage of unending questions, Leanne focused to the extent that she began to develop tunnel vision. Her vision truly became a tunnel, with no signs of light. She became more resentful, more aggressive, her actions became profoundly biased, and the more she behaved erratically, the more people avoided her, and the more she felt deeply misunderstood. Her depression was like the sun—blinding and radiating through to her core.

On a fateful Friday, after writing her last letter to the world, she sat with a Botox-mixed mango juice. It will only hurt for a short time, she thought, until she heard a radio jingle calling out to her. "Come discover yourself at your weakest point...suicide is not the answer."

It was a cliche, yes, but it was said earnestly enough. It probably won't work, she thought. "But let me try it out," she said.

"The Enneagram," the radio blared. And Leanne lost interest a little. Was it simply another tunnel to wander through? The last tunnel she entered got her stuck with nothing to show for it, so how could something called the Enneagram possibly work? Is this just another spirituality phase that will pass?

All these doubts kept her on her toes day and night. Readers, you can't judge her for her ignorance. Affliction, they say, makes a wise man mad. In her case, she wasn't wise enough to be mad—but was feeling insane enough to see through things, hopefully in search of wisdom. All until she was introduced to the Enneagram by her psychologist friend (PS: who also saved her from her second suicide attempt).

A strong and powerful gateway to discovering oneself, the Enneagram has, for decades, served as a powerful tool for the personal and collective transformation of both individuals and groups. Through the Enneagram, Leanne came to terms with the universal language of the world. She learned how to treat and accept herself and others for who they are. The Enneagram, as she learned, could be instrumental in shaping a person's worldview, and the perspective through which they see the world and the people around them. Indeed, most people's core beliefs are not necessarily flawed, but are limiting. Instead, by mastering the Enneagram, Leanne was made to understand that though race and color make us distinct, all humans are unique and share common experiences.

Speaking of experiences, the journey to discovery is just the beginning of a fruitful one. Thus, Leanne's discovery of the Enneagram marked a successful journey in her life, one marked as the reawakening of her full potential. This time, there was a path to the greatness for which she truly longed.

The Enneagram was made for Leanne and she was greatly impacted by it. Leanne wants you (yes, you) and the world to kow about it. Leanne is a writer. Leanne is me and I am Leanne!

So, dearest reader, this book is made to expose you to an in-depth analysis on the Enneagram as a transformative personality tool. It will have practical insights and you will learn how it works along with the keys to discovering oneself. It will cover the challenges in keeping up consistently with good behavior and attitude, and teach you to control your stress patterns. Lastly, it will present a stakeholders' analysis of this tool (what you stand to gain after achieving mastery of this tool).

I must confess that it is a long way to discovering oneself, so do not assume that by just reading this book, you'll suddenly already know yourself. Not so! However, this book will become part of the essential tools you'll need to do so. Taking care of your mental and physical health is also another key. Engaging the services of a competent psychologist, attempting verified personality tests, and, more importantly, properly training your mindset and beliefs should guarantee you smooth sailing to the voyage of self-discovery.

As promised, this book will be insightful and entertaining. Yes, I know learning about the Enneagram isn't always easy, and it's a continually ongoing process, but it's worth it. Have no fear or reluctance, as this book will simplify virtually everything you need to know about this tool. In my view, your journey to self-discovery will be smoother than mine. So let's jump on the train as you flip the next page.

Your friend in the Enneagram school,

Leanne Walters,

Origin of the Enneagram

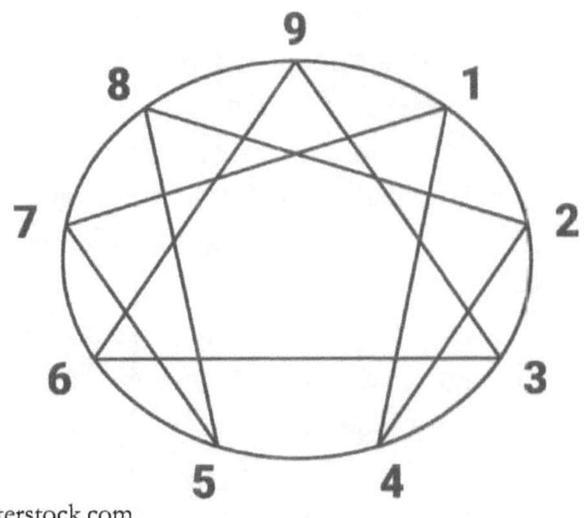

Source: shutterstock.com

What is the Enneagram?

Dearest Reader,

Have you ever thought that you would never reach your full potential? Or have you ever felt like in some ways your actions were sabotaging and self-destructive to yourself or others, despite your good intentions? And now, are you faced with these questions: "How do I create and work the changes I've always longed for? How do I identify and hone my personality to find the true path to my passion and destiny?"

Well, the Enneagram is here for you!

The Enneagram is a system of personality models that helps guide and interpret people's day to day interactions with the world. It is a mirror of reflection where people can see through their emotions and their motivations as a means to giving them the edge to conquer their sins and fears. Through its symbols, wings, and types, people become enlightened and put themselves on the path to self-discovery as well as having better interactions with people in different spheres of their lives.

Although the concept of the Enneagram looks captivating, imagine divergent views from different schools of thought disputing one another. Funnily enough, the reason for their dispute is centered on the origin of the Enneagram and its development. However, our job is not to pick which school of thought is right or wrong. Rather, in the course of pure education, we shall bear the responsibility to vividly discuss every idea and work of art. We shall also look at its journey through history and how it became established, starting with the Medieval Period.

Medieval Period (4th Century)

At this time, religion was the order of the day. Whether it was Sufi or Christianity, each religion was continually finding ways to appeal to their subjects' psychological state and spirituality. Therefore, the Enneagram in this era was connected to different spiritual and oral traditions, as well as specific geometry and mathematical traditions.

For instance, some schools of thought claimed that the Enneagram could be traced to the sacred Pythagoras theorem (invented by Pythagoras and Euclid). In Christian society, mystic writers, such as Plotinus in his book *Enneads,* speak extensively about how nine divine qualities are manifest in human nature. Another writer named Philo, in his thesis on esoteric Judaism, extols a mystic tree called the "Nine-Foldedness of the tree of life in Kabbalah."

Aside from promoting their works, variations of these sects had symbols to propagate messages relevant to Enneagram study. For instance, the Judaism sect had the Star of David (which present-day scholars refer to as a model of growth, maturity, traumatic shock, and heroism). The Sufi brotherhood likewise had a nine-shaped symbol in their Naqshbandi (Brotherhood of the Bees) order.

Renaissance Period

This era was marked by a craving for knowledge, including scientific observations (behaviorism/empiricism) and literary works that spurred thought-providing renditions for readers at that time. Celebrated works that came out of this period include the Sufi use of algebraic geometry (largely introduced by Muhammad ibn Musa al-Khwarizmi) to unravel psychological and spiritual facts among their adherents as well as for business purposes.

The literary era saw a rise of writers and their works, including Homer's *The Odyssey* and, more typically, Dante's *Divine Comedy*, which shares similarities to the study of the Enneagram. In *The Odyssey*, the protagonist, Odysseus, visits nine mythic lands after his ill-fated victory in the Trojan Wars. In his quest, he encounters nine locals whose traits are highly synonymous with the nine Enneagram types. It is worth knowing that the order of the visits was in direct accordance with the order of the Enneagram symbol. Hence, the book was an accurate representation of a journey to one's true self.

Dante's *Divine Comedy*, on the other hand, seeks to introduce three cardinal segments of Hell, Purgatory, and Heaven, which directly references a trinity. He gave strong credence to the Enneagram when he introduced the theme of "Waking up in a Dark Wood", in which he subtly gave the essence of the Enneagram as a transformative tool for one's personality. The mention of unique numbers, such as the seven gates of sin and the nine points in the diagram, likewise speaks of an approach to the Enneagram.

Modern Era (The 21st Century Enneagram)

The recent evolution of the Enneagram is much clearer in the form and shape known in the 21st century. Gurdjieff, a Russian mystic and teacher, used the Enneagram to explain the unfolding of creation, calling it a symbol of perpetual motion. Movements, or sacred dances, constitute an integral part of the Gurdjieff Work. Gurdjieff sometimes referred to himself as a "teacher of dancing." He alludes to the fact that he was introduced to the Enneagram in the 1920s during a visit to a monastery in Afghanistan. Still, he does not definitively explain the symbol's origin. Nathan Bernier describes him thus:

"Indirectly, in a manner as invisible and anonymous as the heroes of the French resistance, his seeds infiltrated the contemporary ideological currents about man and the universe. He was a pioneering environmentalist, showing, in the Ray of Creation, the place that man occupies in the unique organism of the Organic Life on Earth. The astonishing simplicity of his explanations of the laws governing the world has been accepted by some of the most obstinate scientific minds. His methods for Work on oneself, self-knowledge, and the harmonious development of man's three centers (mental, physical, and emotional) have provided new and solid bases for modern psychological therapies and the entire new science of self-help."

In South America, Oscar Ichazo, the Bolivian-born founder of the Arica School that he established in 1968, also taught the Enneagram. During the 1960s, Ichazo's Enneagram of Personality and related theories formed part of a larger body of teaching that he termed Protoanalysis.

Claudio Naranjo, a Chilean psychiatrist, was exposed to the Enneagram through Ichazo and brought the Enneagram into the modern psychological tradition. Individuals such as Ochs, Almaas, and Maitri studied with Naranjo, who still teaches the Enneagram to this day. Through Ochs, the Enneagram was introduced to numerous

Christian communities in the United States, where authors such as Wagner, Riso, and Hudson were exposed to the teachings.

Since its introduction into the world of psychology, the Enneagram has been partially validated through experiential and empirical studies (for a summary, see Sutton 2012). It has also been cross-referenced with other constructs of psychology such as the MBTI. Enneagram teachers have also drawn on the work of psychologists outside the Enneagram community to enhance our understanding and application of the framework. One example is the work of Karen Horney on psychological forms of defense, which has led to Riso and Hudson developing the fractal pattern of the Hornevians, or social styles.

We acknowledge the rich contributions of all the Enneagram authors and practitioners that have contributed to our cumulative understanding and continue to inspire our application of the Enneagram.

Facts about the Enneagram

Everyone thinks deciphering the Enneagram is as easy as that of zodiac signs (it's not!). Others see it as a conspiracy theory only believed by rednecks. But the bittersweet truth lies in the fact that it takes a long time to grasp the borders of the Enneagram, as it cuts across all borders—from spirituality to business, then to social life. It's rigid, but at the same time its flexibility speaks volumes of its dexterity and versatility in the hands of the learned. At the same time, it's a complex and confusing model to apply in one's endeavors.

Here are salient findings addressing these facts as well as distinguishing them from myths or conspiracy theories.

Enneagram Myths
Myth 1: You can be more than one number.

People so often think that they can pick and mix their numbers. Sometimes people like to cherry-pick the personality they want to be by dipping into different numbers. I have heard one person claim she's a bit of a Number 4 and 8 mixed together. I hate to spoil the fun, but while it would certainly be interesting to pull a little bit of energy from the strengths of all the numbers of the Enneagram (that is, only if we understand the nature of these strengths), true Enneagram wisdom teaches us unequivocally that "everyone is one core number on the Enneagram", and blending into another number is our body's response to the triads (Instinct, Intuition, and Intellect). This leads us to the concept of the nature and values model.

Truth: Nature and Values Model

Definitively, the Enneagram model focuses more on nature and values rather than a single personality type or reductive behaviors. In short, it draws from many sources, including ancient wisdom, traditions, and modern psychology to help people understand their values and unique survival strategies.

For example, the Enneagram Personality Type Seven, which is associated with enthusiasm, is used to describe one who has an innate capacity and desire for enthusiasm and adventure as well as someone who is keen to derive value from experience. As such, the phrase "I am an Enthusiast" could be changed to "I value experiences", which gives insight into the intrinsic nature of the Seven personality type and at the same time begs the question, "What else do they value?"'

Therefore, the versatile Enneagram creates self-awareness and helps us discover the patterns of behavior that subconsciously motivate us to act in certain ways. When we become conscious of these patterns and motivations, we can transcend them and develop richer, more supportive ways of being ourselves. We have to understand that ultimately, the Enneagram is important as a way of determining one's type and coming to fully know and understand one's focus of attention, core beliefs, defense mechanisms, alternative coping strategies, and path to development. The objectivity of the Enneagram's value emanates from identifying one's type that is not based on external behaviors, but from a more in-depth understanding of how behavioral patterns relate to one's focus of attention, motivation, strategies, and personal experience. This is precisely what Socrates meant by saying, "Know thyself."

To provide a clearer picture of this assertion, it is essential to note that each number on the Enneagram is determined by a specific sin, motivation, and desire (SMD). All the sins, motivations, and desires for each number are vastly different. Enneagram wisdom teaches that you can't vacillate between two numbers, which is why we have the single-model mantra. That is to say, you have one core number that is connected (via dynamic movement) to four other numbers.

Myth 2: You can be a "tie of numbers."

This is a catchy phrase that is very prevalent in the media these days. Take an online Enneagram assessment; some places give you an answer that is more of a ranking for each number to which you might be connected. It might be a result like "75% Seven, 15% Eight, 10% Five", with the caption stating that you are "A three-way tie of an Enthusiast/Epicurean (7), Boss/Challenger (8), and an Observer (5)." This is a big misunderstanding of the workings of the Enneagram.

Truth: Tie of Numbers.

Indeed, one could be a blend of these three numbers, but, as mentioned before, you only have one true core Enneagram number. It is true that you could be identified with more than one number, yet the Enneagram doesn't change, and neither does our core number (also referred to as our basic type). Nor can we choose our number. In most cases, it could be through genetics or a centric nature that you developed through childhood, either through fear or burning desire. Still, in the same vein, our number doesn't change. Being our basic number type, it is the same today as when we were children, and it will stay the same for the rest of our lives.

Myth 4: "My number is better than yours."

Sometimes when we read about these numbers and their specific attributes, we fall in love with the numbers. But with love can come hate—in this case, hatred toward other numbers. So you may hear people saying:

"I want no stress, I want to be with a better number…preferably a number seven."

"Oh, I'm a number four, I'm the best number you could get. I mean, I'm so romantic (eat your heart out, Frank Ocean)."

"I can never be attached to a number three…these days it's all about money or nothing!"

Truth: "My number is better than yours."

"One man's poison is another man's meat."

The world we live in is unbalanced, just like our nature. All numbers have their unique attributes as well as their sins. So does choosing one element from the other not create inequality in the same unbalanced system?

McDonough agrees about the danger of using the Enneagram system to flatten ourselves or others using types or numbers.

"The Enneagram should not be used to stereotype others, draw premature conclusions, put other people down, flaunt your knowledge of their flaws in an argument, fire someone, or any other action that would be hurtful or abrupt and conclusive." - McDonough

Here are some practical examples to show you all numbers, using the types Three, Four, and Nine.

To start, the Three is referred to as "The Achiever." Everyone wants to be associated with this number because they want to achieve things in their life. However, the sin associated with this number is deceit. Threes can be so good at deceiving themselves (and others) that they often can't handle it. In fact, a lot of the time they don't even know how they feel about their achievements. Although they may feel what everyone else feels, it's only a yardstick to help them get to the top of whatever their current obstacle(s) might be. This obstacle may involve either work, a personal experience, or a relationship. With this characteristic exhibited, they might be seen as opportunists or referred to in derogatory language such as "gold-diggers" because, with their innate character, they cannot actually connect with other people in a meaningful way.

So let's circle back to your original thoughts of an Achiever. Do you want to be that way, or have friends or relationships that are like that? Because it's not wholly flattering, is it?

A Four is often called a Romantic or an Individualist. Again, these sweet words have very positive connotations in our minds because somewhere inside, we all would like to be lovers (without the heartbreak). We'd all like to be the recipient or giver of romance, and we would all like to find a meaningful lifelong relationship. However, when you take into account that our Four's sin is being green with envy, and that they are always longing after what others have, while still wanting to remain as unique as they are, you can see how that can quickly become a confusing way to live.

And finally, a nine is called a Peacemaker or Mediator, which sounds lovely, and we could certainly use more of them in today's society. However, a nine's primary desire is to avoid all conflict, at any cost, including avoiding life situations and relationships that might cause conflict, which can lead to isolation. So, a Nine—even an opinionated Nine— will hold their opinions to themselves and merge with others to avoid any conflict. This ultimately means that they aren't really making peace between others, but are avoiding life to avoid conflict. Do you see that marked difference?

One of the biggest life hacks and lessons the Enneagram can teach you is how to appreciate people for who they truly are irrespective of their bad character traits, and, at the same time, how to constantly work on yourself to become a better you.

Study of the Enneagram

Self-Development Using the Enneagram

"As a man thinketh, so is he."

At what point do our endeavors fail? This can reveal our chief feature that cannot be overcome, according to Gurdjieff. Observe and write down the point at which you tend to get frustrated or paralyze your activities, and how you justify this. In the beginning, we need to turn off old associations and ask at each point: Where is my mistake? Where did I wander?

You could ask questions like:

1. What did I want?

Passive 1 (7-1) — Which model inspired me? How did I see the object of my desire?

Active 1 (1-4) — How did I imagine it would be in the physical world?

2. Did I plan explicitly? Did I evaluate the pros and cons? Did I try to learn something before beginning?

Passive 2 (4-2) — How did I interpret material limitations?

Active 2 (2-8) — Did I establish a goal? Did I quantify it? Did I develop deadlines and timelines? Did I consult the market? Did I consult more experienced people?

3. Did I provoke or take advantage of the first shock to leave the mental plan and to involve myself with the material actualization of the idea? Did I notice and welcome the first shock that was given to me by life?

4. Did I structure and organize the activities and input physically, in relation to space and time? Did I persist in the necessary routine activities that are at times boring, but essential?

Passive 4 (1-4) — Did I carry out the routine work always inspired by the initial will? Or did I become a slave, identifying with the routine, and let myself deviate to wherever chance would take me?

Active 4 (4-2) — Did I feed and reprogram my plans with the data found in the material world, which could alter the initial plan?

5. Did I have enough courage and presence of mind to execute the required action at the right moment, leaving the preparation routines and facing the irreversible process? Did I transform anything?

Passive 5 (8-5) — At the moment of action, did I remain receptive to the goal, the experience, the market, the client, and the further use of my work?

Active 5 (5-7) — Did I act with responsibility, thinking about the consequences of my actions, the final goal, how it would be when finished, and how it could inspire others?

6. Did I have enough courage to perceive the moment to halt the action and go on to the stage of real sharing? Was I brave enough to finish the work

and involve myself personally with the consequences, to face the losses resulting from this, to face the gains, to face a possible failure or a possible success?

7. Did I consolidate the object of my desire as a ready and real thing, able to serve in turn as a model for others or the next cycle? Did I clear the workplace? Did I throw the remains away? Did I arrange the room?

Passive 7 (5-7) — In the stage of the final presentation of the product, did I respect the execution processes and the material constraints? Did I package it according to its physical characteristics? Or did I get so wrapped up in perfectionism to the point of making it impossible to complete the project?

Active 7 (7-1) — Did I work enough on the final presentation and divulgation of the product?

8. Did I persevere until I completed all the stages of the work, and was I altruistic enough to share my work with others?

Passive 8 (2-8) — Did I respect the initial plans, so that the end could correspond to the beginning? Was there a deviation from the goal, or did I accomplish what was planned? Did I allow myself to be inspired appropriately by the needs of the market? Did I pay attention to the apprentices who came to me? Did I teach what I have learned?

Active 8 (8-5) — Am I ready to guide the activities in the physical world, based on the experience I have acquired? Do I know how to command when it is necessary? Am I able to recognize and even to promote the law of cause and effect?

9. When I felt my work was completed in a finished cycle, was I able to leave? Did I capture the

essence of this experience? Did I recognize that the end of a cycle is just the seed for the beginning of another, higher cycle? Am I willing to begin again, at the same level?

Mental Stages

There is no time or space. The world of ideas is relatively easy, fed by imagination at all levels. Although not real, it is rich and varied in possibilities. Nothing seems to be asked by us. If I want to build a house, in my thoughts, I can have many houses at the same time—houses of different types, sizes, and styles. I can have several professions, skills, and talents.

Danger of 1: Indecision. Point 1 lives in the imagination of several possibilities. The mind swarms with creativity. The danger is not facing the restrictions imposed by the necessary choice to develop one idea (2). Escaping from 1. Going back to 9 □. Laziness and self-compliance. Stagnation. Jumping to 4 □. Instead of just consulting 4 planning (1-4-2), falling directly into and getting stuck in routine, maintenance and detail activities. Since 4 needs material (3), this path of falling many times is traced as 1-3-4: having ideas and going straight to the physical world, buying things, acquiring materials; then continuing in eternal physical preparation, without strength for actually executing. Then, at any new inspiration, we retrace the path 1-3-4, being imprisoned there. Moving forward incomplete to 2 □. Going ahead and jumping immediately into planning, time charting and allocation of resources without verifying the practical feasibility of the idea (1-4), or when we do not yet really know what we want (7-1).

Danger of 2: Imagination. Once one idea is chosen among several others, the commitment for its accomplishment is still at the level of thoughts and words. This is a Mi interval. We need something from the outer world, demanding real action. Point 2 puts the idea on paper, makes calculations, and simulates all stages of the process. It develops the idea. If the idea is a house, what is it for? To live in? To rent? To sell? This choice will determine the specifications of the project, the budget, and the timescale. Action is required, but the project can dwell here indefinitely, in playful planning activity. Escaping from 2. Going back to 1 □. After verifying its feasibility (1-4-2), returning and doubting the initial idea or the established goal; deciding to aim for something else, or aiming for anything. Jumping to 8 □. Trying to harvest without planting. Thinking we already know everything and wanting to teach without having learned. Moving forward incomplete to 3 □. Going ahead and making arrangements in the material world before having completed the necessary stage of 2, for instance, acquiring material before defining what is needed.

Danger of 3: Procrastination. Here, procrastination becomes evident. Time begins to matter; however, the material world attracts us and it seems to matter more than time itself. Escaping from 3. Going back to 2 □. Postponing the commitment to enter the physical world, dwelling in illusion and mental fantasy. Being delighted with planning and never moving on to execution. Jumping to 6 □. Trying to involve other people immediately in the process, assuming premature emotional commitments and making hurried decisions, when nothing has begun yet—counting the chicks before they hatch—moving forward incomplete to 4 □. Getting into the routine before having the necessary structure, and becoming dependent.

Physical Stages

Besides being rather complicated, the physical stage is very deceiving because most people think it is the last one and that any accomplishment in the material realm is enough.

Danger of 4: Detail and Anonymity. Analytical, concerned with details, Point 4 can get lost in eternal perfectionism, missing the forest for the trees. On the other hand, the better the work of 4, the less the author appears. The main danger of 4 is wishing to appear, and to accomplish this, it relaxes its functions, getting more attention through absence than through presence. We remember the cook when dinner does not appear on the table, and the storeroom boss is called when there is no paper for the copier. Escaping from 4. Going back to 1 □. Trying to escape from routine work, influenced by the force of 1, creating new ideas—therefore, going against the initial idea, which was the basis of the present work—going back to 2 □. Always wanting to reprogram. Reprogramming is a natural movement, but should not be used to alter the routine continuously. This happens with very creative people, who receive a strong impulse from 1 (1-4-2)—moving forward incomplete to 5 ☐. Beginning to execute the main action without the necessary supporting preparation. The inopportune passage from 4 to 5 is harmful to the whole process. In this passage, transformation is irreversible, and the price to be paid for precipitation at this point is high. Usually, the cause is the desire to escape from anonymity and to appear.

Danger of 5: Activism. Here, there is the same risk of automatism that there was at 4; however, this time with the illusion of accomplishment. There is the danger of remaining in activity because of pure mechanical inertia. Further, as 5 transforms material irreversibly, there will be damage if the process is not completed. A good example is when we are painting a picture and do not know when to stop, so a single additional brushstroke can destroy everything. It is necessary to recognize the moment to stop. Escaping from 5. Going back to 4 ☐. Returning to preparation and support stages instead of accomplishing the main action, either due to incompetence or to a perfectionism that hinders any achievement—never feeling prepared enough for the responsibility. It is like the son who, after becoming an independent adult, returns to live with his parents—jumping to 7. Hastily ending a task that is not finished yet in order to be free from the work. Moving forward incomplete to 6 ☐. This is very rare, due to the Harnel-Aoot. The premature emotional involvement at this point is due to a great illusion about oneself, with a lot of self-sacrifice and losses, or overestimating one's real power.

Danger of 6: Fear. If nature helps in the first interval, at this point, it does the opposite. Moreover, the higher the goal, the more difficulties will appear—because of the cosmic homeostasis. In self-development, this is the portal at which we see ourselves as we really are. Occultist schools call this "the threshold" and say that here we face the "terror of the threshold": ourselves. No matter what the process is in which we are involved, it is impossible not to see ourselves when passing correctly through 6. At 5, we have the options of living by the pentagram normally or upside down. However, at 6, we must harmonize its light side with its dark side, as in Solomon's Seal. Some people "declare" their own victory or defeat early—they crystallize a positive or negative self-image and spend the rest of their lives trying to confirm it. The only word God knows is "Yes."

I knew an architect who has declared himself a "victim of life," thinking life always owes him something—and he didn't get to conclude his own house, letting it turn into ruin when there was just a little effort lacking to complete it. He didn't get to face the 6, his transformation, because he would pass from being a "victim" to a "happy proprietor" and a successful professional. With his experience, I began to understand better the Harnel-Aoot. Many psychological aspects of the second octave Mi are added to the first octave Sol, demanding a conscious shock in this interval. It is common to receive "negative shocks" from the descending movement of the Ray of Creation, which goes down with all its potency at this point. This is good, because it does not allow things to stand still. The adverse shocks can be transformed into conscious shocks by intentional acceptance. From the point of view of the individual, the adverse shock can initially seem to be the opposite of help, but in cosmic terms, it is an effort against stagnation. You must react to it in one way or another: either you fight or you die. We should be thankful for difficulties, since only with them can we become strong and grow. Escaping from 6. Going back to 5 □. Once the execution stage is finished, the danger of going back or continuing "doing" after being ready, without submitting to the transformation. Jumping to 9 □. Deceiving oneself, thinking that finishing the main action is to complete the process. By dropping things in the middle, it will be practically impossible to continue them afterwards. Moving forward, incomplete to 7 □. Daring to declare ready and resolved what is not yet prepared. Presenting oneself as a winner without deserving it. It is like the premature birth of a baby.

Emotional Stages

Starting at 6, commitment and thus responsibility is demanded. They are for the good or for the bad. If there is no consciousness and intention, a descending "default" will be assumed. Gurdjieff explained this well in relation to nutrition: some higher energies, if not used for building higher bodies, will go back in an evolutionary process, causing illness and shortening of life.

Danger of 7: Isolation. The work is ready, clean, and beautiful—and again, we have the illusion of something that is finished. No. It is not finished yet.

A work needs to be seen, shared, and used. Actually, this is not difficult, because here there is no interval and the work itself, if finished with success, will provide the necessary energy to continue. Escaping from 7. Going back to 5 ☐. Being stuck in a victim's role or attached to personality. Having a fear of appearing as a winner or of losing the executioner's status. Jumping to 1 ☐. Beginning other things or trying different versions of the same idea, diving into a new activity without having accomplished the previous one. Thus, the process is self-feeding, and the author is imprisoned in the 7-1 area. Moving forward incomplete to 8 ☐. This is like selling a product without packaging it, or eating without a plate in a dirty kitchen. Complementary actions have not been accomplished, so the work cannot be left just sitting there or be praised.

Danger of 8: Ingratitude. The work was presented, offered, and celebrated. It is necessary to thank and pay all debts. It is essential to share the experience. Escaping from 8. Going back to 7 ☐. Hesitation in leading, in passing on what we have learned, or assuming our own maturity to benefit others. Fear of losing the position achieved, not recognizing that a higher class is now offered. Fear of karmic reaction and of suffering the effects it has caused. Jumping to 2 ☐. Not assuming the higher social position, not assuming that your future is happening now. Instead of teaching, studying even more. The eternal student and the eternal planner are imprisoned in the 2-8 area. Moving forward incomplete to 9 ☐. Retiring from the process while you still have commitments to it. Ignoring quality control and client satisfaction, not worrying about the outcomes, the storage of this experience, or the energy for the next cycle.

Danger of 9: Status Quo. Process completed. Resting before a new cycle. The very satisfaction with the achievement is the biggest danger here. The individual thinks he "is already done" and can now stop. No. He cannot control. Escaping from 9. Going back to 8 □. Wanting to keep the position of being the responsible party and leader, refusing to withdraw at the moment the position should be left for those who are younger or others that follow. The individual becomes the largest obstacle to his own work and also for the next cycle. Jumping to 3 □. Childish attitudes when maturity demands responsibility. Improper use of the goods received. Hesitation in assuming the natural leadership of age or development. Moving forward incomplete to forgetting that resting is as necessary to begin a new cycle as Sunday is to the week. Not respecting natural limits. Denying oneself the task of irradiating the influence of the power achieved.

Personal Management

Everything that is created has to be maintained and good maintenance means administration. If we do this with the company, the car, and other things we have, why don't we also administer it to ourselves intentionally and technically? The Work is, actually, technology. The way of spiritual development begins when there has already been personal development in ordinary life. It is not for people with psychological problems—therefore, if you need to, you must seek specialized help in advance. It is also not for people who don't know how to support themselves materially in life. So we must study and have a profession before entering the spiritual way.

Even after joining an esoteric school, your ordinary life should continue and it will be more difficult because you will live two parallel lives. So—study, find teachers, read books in your regular daily life, and use the Enneagram to affirm yourself before and after entering the spiritual way.

"Be in the world without being of the world."

What the Enneagram Teaches Us

Dearest Reader,

Life is like a journey; you pass through phases...just like you're reading through the chapters of this book. You are now in the second portal to rediscover yourself.

In this chapter, you shall be exposed to the conceptual types of the Enneagram, how they manifest, and the distinctive character traits they possess. You'll also learn the other, darker side of each type's characteristics.

Hence, we shall vividly discuss the anatomy of man's inner triangle (the three centers of human existence), which leads to the nine personality types of the Enneagram, as well as giving you detailed descriptions of them. We will also show you steps on how to identify your personality type and what to do after discovering yourself.

Anatomy of Man and the Enneagram

Man is a three-brained being. In other words, he has three centers or independent brains with different functions and manifestations: the physical, the emotional, and the intellectual. Just like the mechanism of the Horse, Carriage, and Rider, there would be glaring anomalies if any of them goes missing. For instance, if the horse goes missing, no means for transportation; if the carriage is missing, no means to carry essential goods; and when the rider is missing…we now have bigger problems.

Applying this trio to the human mechanism sees them as being so interwoven that any missing piece could lead to a dysfunctional human being. It is with this anatomy that we derive our nine personality types where we can rank our instincts, emotions, and our intellectual capacity.

Understanding the Nine Personality Types

The Enneagram personality types

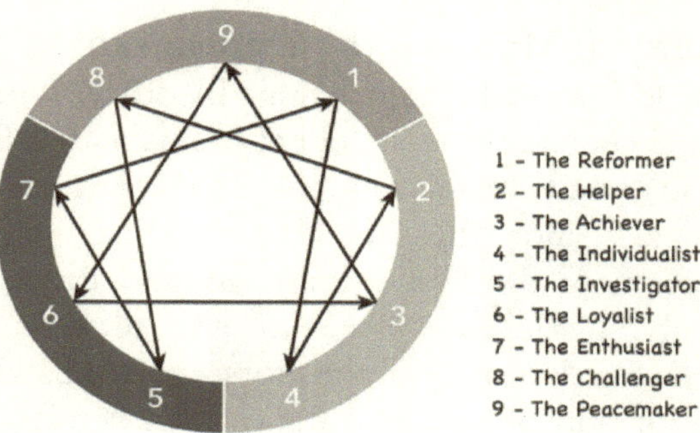

Source: shutterstock.com

Overview

Basically, the Enneagram model consists of a nine-type system based on separate psychological aspects. According to this system, each of the nine personality types is defined and represented by a particular core belief about how they see the world around them (in terms of interests, relationships, spirituality, politics, etc.). This core belief not only grants foresight, but shapes a person's view and the perspective through which they see the world while offering the necessary approach to the people around them. Just like a rogue lawyer accusing a thief of burglary when he himself has willfully tampered evidence to win court cases, our core beliefs are not necessarily incorrect, but they are limiting. So we must train ourselves to never be vindictive and assertive over another person's life. But understanding our Enneagram type and how it paints our perceptions can help us broaden our perspective.

And with reasonable empathy and logic, we can approach situations more effectively.

Understanding a person's Enneagram type can be likened to a movie we crave to watch. Some of us do not like spoiler alerts, but through flashbacks, suspenseful scenes, and a bit of soliloquy, we can anticipate what will happen to the lead character. Whether good or bad luck may befall them, we have already seen both the remote and immediate factors that have led to the outcome, just as we know Voldemort is plotting against Harry Potter and his friends simply because while they were away, Voldemort was placing spells on his portal to block them.

Applying this illustration to the Enneagram places us in the position of an omniscient audience as it helps us anticipate people's behavioral tendencies and gives us empathy to see and analyze why they behave the way they do. Each Enneagram type has a set of core beliefs/principles that does the dual work of enabling them to make certain decisions and, at the same time, motivating them to take particular actions. These behavioral traits may seem positive, negative, confusing or contradictory. Yet, the very fact that each trait can often be explained shows the relevance of the Enneagram in helping us understand one's type.

Personality Phases

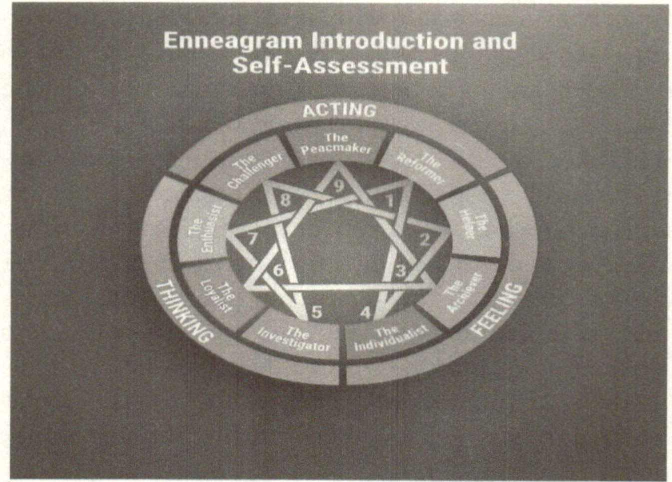

Source: shutterstock.com

The Enneagram is a chart of personalities that seeks to describe people in terms of nine types and gives an in-depth analysis of each type on the basis of the type's motivations, fears, and internal dynamics. Being so in-depth, the Enneagram is seen as an emotionally centered system of understanding people. Each of the nine types of the Enneagram has its own driving force, which is centered around a particular triangular motion called emotional personality phases. Some personality types experience strong emotions while other types are highly resistant and aim to avoid emotions in one form or another. However, whether we choose to ignore our emotions or embrace them wholly, each type prescribes some aspect of emotional experience that, in many cases, overwhelms us.

The nine types of the Enneagram are divided among feeling types, thinking types, and acting types. Feeling types depend on their emotional intelligence to understand their own reactions and connect with others. Thinking types depend on their intellectual intelligence to make sense of things and navigate the world around them. Acting types depend on their instinctual intelligence to follow their gut, and respond to threats and opportunities. In the next section, we will vividly and fully explain each type.

The Acting/Physical or Instinctive Type Etymology

The physical center is the best organized center in an ordinary person. The physical center has been functioning since conception and is responsible for the day to day running of the physical body mechanism, including regulating the accumulation and expenditure of energies. The instinctive functions are unconditional, or more like an automatic default setting as the physical center carries out body functions such as the autonomous internal work of breathing, circulation, digestion, glandular functions, etc. This work also includes automatically maintaining organic life, the senses, and all physical sensations (from the indifferent to both pleasant and unpleasant ones).

When it's in dire straits, the body switches to the instinct of fulfilling basic needs. That is, only external instinctive functions are reflexes as they encompass all external movements, such as walking, jumping, eating, speaking, and writing. However, the automatic actions that one performs without consciousness are not necessarily the instinctive or moving functions; take, for example, the automatic feelings or thoughts based on associations with the past (that are also called reflexes).

The Enneagram and Acting/Physical or Instinctive Type

Since Acting types react with instinct, reflex, or gut feeling, they connect with other people based on their physical sense of comfort (body language) and connect to the world by sensing their body's reaction to what is happening. Acting types include the specific numbers below:

Type One: The REFORMER

With personal integrity and self-control, this type places a lot of emphasis on following the rules and doing things correctly. Their default settings are doing the right thing and shunning the bad, even if it may be at odds with them. They can smell evil, which is a strong attribute.

Type Eight: The CHALLENGER

With their strong energy stemming from enthusiasm and intense power, Eights see themselves as strong and powerful, and they seek to stand up for what they believe in. They command an intimidating body language that makes them good picks for leadership roles. Their body attribute is related to gyrations and high energy.

Type Nine: The PEACEMAKER

Nines are fluid, adaptable, and like to go with the flow and let the people around them set the agenda just for the sake of peace.

Emotional Center

The emotional or affective center is the fastest way to trigger our sensual motions to the world. Yet, this center is not always entirely developed or practical, and can cause us to read the world around us incorrectly (which is why it is not advisable to "think" with one's emotions). In essence, the emotional center allows us to appreciate and evaluate everything in relation to ourselves—namely, in relation to what we notice and know of ourselves. Through it, we usually feel "partial" emotions—that is to say, emotions of only one note: happiness, rage, surprise, etc. These emotions directly affect the physical center, altering the muscular tension and the chemistry of the body. Ordinary emotions, inherent in only one aspect of the individual, are automatic and reactive; they depend on the present and can change easily. A dog, for instance, can have the same ordinary emotions we have, but cannot "love his enemy", which is a real feeling that belongs to the higher emotional center.

In terms of higher feelings, such as real love, we have only rapid glimpses—real love is indivisible, so if we are divided, and if we do not love all and everything, we do not love anything. Gurdjieff uses a special term called "external considering" to designate the kind of conscious love we are able to feel, which also includes respect, compassion, benevolence, and other partial components of love. Therefore, the development of the emotional center is the main goal of esoteric work. It is the key to evolution.

The Feeling Types of the Enneagram

Feeling types react with emotions first. They connect with other people on an empathetic level and make sense of the world by understanding their feelings about it.

Type Two: The HELPER
Twos want to be liked and find ways that they can be helpful to others so that they can belong.

Type Three: The ACHIEVER
Threes want to be successful and admired by other people, and so are very conscious of their public image.

Type Four: The INDIVIDUALIST
Fours want to be unique and to experience deep, authentic emotions.

Intellectual or Mental Center

Being the slowest of all, the intellectual center—or the function of thought—performs mental processes such as perception of impressions, formation of ideas, representations, concepts, reasoning, comparisons, affirmations, denial, formation of words, language, imagination, etc. The mental center allows us to compare, to judge, to plan, to coordinate, to classify, and to foresee. Initially empty, it goes through intense development soon after birth.

In our civilization, this center has received the most training and is sometimes hypertrophied, though it's also true that nowadays the physical center is receiving more and more attention.

The Thinking Types of the Enneagram

Thinking types react with analysis first. They connect with other people on an intellectual level and make sense of the world by understanding the systems and theories that underlie what they observe.

Type Five: The INVESTIGATOR

Fives seek understanding and knowledge, and are more comfortable with data than other people.

Type Six: The LOYALIST

Sixes are preoccupied with security, seek safety, and like to be prepared for problems.

Type Seven: The ENTHUSIAST

Sevens want to have as much fun and adventure as possible and are easily bored.

Observations of the Nine Personality Types

Type One

Ones are defined by their desire to do things correctly and to avoid being wrong or making mistakes. To others, they appear perfectionistic, responsible, and exacting. Ones are typically sticklers for rules and details, and get frustrated when they are not given the opportunity to make sure things are up to their very high standards.

Ones fear being flawed or imperfect, and cope with this fear by being very strict with themselves. They are always striving, and seeking the best and most correct way to do things.

Defining Characteristics of the Enneagram Type One

- Serious and straightforward during conversation
- Attuned to practicality and frugality
- Hardworking and diligent as employees
- High internal standards

- Rigidity in plans and decisions
- Intense ability to concentrate
- Natural talent for teaching and instructing

What Are Reformers Like?

Reformers are responsible and serious-minded pragmatists. They seek to improve the welfare of people and make things better for the greater good. To do this, they use their best judgment to find solutions that can be applied in the real world. They have a deep appreciation and interest in ethics, and frequently spend time evaluating and adjusting their moral compass as necessary. Often struck with a crystal-clear life mission, Reformers hustle behind the scenes to transform their powerful vision into reality with a strong sense of duty and tenaciousness. Quiet and controlled, they will follow through with their words and commitments.

Reformers are willing to go the extra mile to ensure their work is top-notch and curated to perfection. They take great pride in crafting streamlined schedules and ways to carry out tasks in the most efficient manner possible—optimization is a lifestyle choice.

What Are the Reformer's Core Values?

Reformers have a set of very high internal standards. They desire to improve every aspect of their lives. They aim for their actions to be consistent with their values and principles, and work extremely hard to do so.

Responsibility and due diligence are the golden pillars of a Reformer's values. They strive for accountability and appreciate the functionality of various products and systems. Integrity is a key factor in their life choices and stands the test of time. Loyalty, justice, and honesty are the core ingredients in shaping a Reformer's down-to-earth character.

How Can I Recognize a Type One?

A clear and organized life, both inside and out, is the Reformer's ultimate goal. Steadfast and diligent, Reformers seek to improve the state of the world through intention and reason. They have a clear sense of duty and feel obligated to serve society through willpower and perseverance.

Their method of communication is typically direct, honest, and deliberate. With little patience for small talk, they take charge of their duties in a contained manner. Fashion trends are of little concern—they prefer to invest in high-quality pieces that'll stand the test of time, with relationships that follow a similar outlook.

With their keen ability to discern, they gravitate toward careers in the military, law, forensics, finance and academia. In the workplace, they carry out tasks carefully and methodologically. A Reformer may be the star employee who goes above and beyond to complete all work to a high standard.

What Are Reformers Like under Different Levels of Health?

At healthy levels: Reformers see an abundance of situations to improve and accept the dynamic chaos of life as it is. They have a strong sense of justice and fairness, and are willing to tolerate and understand the diversity of humanity to make further progress for the greater good. The Reformer achieves an ideal work-life balance and understands how to relax.

At average levels: Reformers organize and compartmentalize all aspects of their lives, follow strict ideals, and are likely passionate about various social causes. This is evident in their professional or personal pursuits and societal memberships. Often rigid workaholics, Reformers may suppress emotional needs in order to get things done.

At unhealthy levels: Reformers become out of touch with reality and focus on irrelevant factors. This can lead to a self-affirming spiral of prejudice to the point of obsession and compulsion. They may discredit others' opinions and nitpick to keep their distorted self-image in check. There is little room for error in this state, and so Reformers can fall into explosions of rage and fury when their principles are under attack.

Type Two

Twos are defined by their desire to belong and to be loved by others. They are helpful, nurturing, and caring towards others. They are eager to involve themselves in others' lives and rarely say no when others ask them for help. They make sure they are important to others by always being there for them.

Twos fear being alone and unloved, and cope with this fear by taking care of others and making themselves central to other people's lives.

Defining Characteristics of the Enneagram Type Two

- Warm smile and eyes
- Approachable and radiates kindness

- Vocal volunteer or activist
- Excellent team player
- Caring and gentle
- Nurturing and patient
- Smooth, flowing movements

What Are Helpers Like?

Helpers are highly empathetic and caring individuals who put others' needs above their own. They have intuitive abilities to anticipate the emotional gaps of others and support them. They find great joy in being available and are seen as a source of encouragement or a shoulder to cry on. Through thick and thin, they're the ride-or-die companion and friend. Usually open and popular, Helpers find themselves in a variety of groups and are liked by many. Their encouraging and supportive nature draws in people from all stages of their lives.

What Are the Helper's Core Values?

A strong sense of meaning, acknowledgment from loved ones, and emotional intimacy with others are the Helper's grounding principles. Altruism holds a strong place in their heart and they readily go out of their way to volunteer their time and energy to bring others up. Kindness and reciprocity are the guiding values of their decisions. They feel that improving someone else's life or mood is immeasurably better than helping themselves. To Helpers, the shared experience of spending quality time with a loved one is among the best feelings in the world.

How Can I Recognize a Type Two?

In public, Helpers are the people to whom strangers are naturally drawn for directions or advice. They possess a strong aura of approachability. They're highly attuned to the needs of others and can be seen as the "mother" or "father" figure of a group of friends. At home or alone, they continually make an effort to keep in touch with loved ones. Whether it's through homemade dishes, tender words, or surprise gifts, they're attuned to others' love languages and enjoy putting a smile on their faces.

What Are Helpers Like under Different Levels of Health?

At healthy levels: Helpers are selfless caregivers who are fulfilled by freely giving unconditional love. They're comfortable with sharing their own needs with others and secure a healthy give-and-take balance. They acknowledge when others require distance and develop secure attachment styles. They're able to practice mindfulness and understand the meaning of altruism. They recognize their own self-worth and can gently guide others toward theirs as well. Helpers understand the meaning of empathy and are able to have genuine, heart-to-heart connections with others.

At average levels: Helpers assume the martyr role in relationships and constantly seek ways to feel important by attending to others' needs. They feel fulfilled when others remind them how grateful they are to have them in their lives, and work hard to maintain this image of the constantly accessible friend. By continuously attending to others' needs, Helpers may burn out and overcompensate for their energy levels. They may use flattery or compliments in order to gain acceptance and appreciation within a community or relationship. They're hypersensitive to the approval and appraisal of others, especially those they truly care about.

At unhealthy levels: Helpers fall into a pit of self-despair and criticism—constantly looking for others' faults and wrongdoings. They try to gain control over relationships and may become overly clingy or overbearing. There's now an excuse for their every action and they play the victim card in order to gain sympathy and reassurance. Finally, they unleash their manipulative side, and mindlessly blame other people for their suffering and misery. Helpers base their self-worth on the opinions of those they've helped—and if received with criticism, they'll wallow in despair and develop various forms of physical illness: aches, fevers, and nausea.

Type Three

Threes are defined by their desire to be significant and to distinguish themselves through their achievements. They are unsure of their innate self-worth and look for validation through their accomplishments. To others, they appear confident, ambitious, and goal-oriented. Threes are typically very image-focused; it is important to them that others see them as successful.

Threes fear being insignificant or a failure. To cope with this fear, they look for ways to win in life, reassuring themselves that they are valuable.

Defining Characteristics of the Enneagram Type Three

- Acutely aware of social niceties

- Impressive range of accomplishments
- Extremely busy and on the go
- Jam-packed schedules and meetings
- May have interests in improvisation or acting
- Refined taste in outer appearance
- Charismatic; makes a good first impression

What Are Achievers Like?

Polished and sophisticated, Achievers have a particular taste for the nicer things in life. They have the capacity for huge chunks of productivity to reach their goals and high standards. Their goal is to be remembered and appreciated for their discoveries and creations—to be the best. Smart, ambitious, and typically well-dressed, Achievers hit and exceed targets left and right. Their performance and dedication is admired by others and may even inspire them to take action. Achievers typically have schedules chock-full of fun events and professional meetings to keep themselves busy and on the go.

What Are the Achiever's Core Values?

Recognition, accolades, and status are the pinnacle of the Achiever's lifestyle. They're goal-driven and equipped with the Type A mentality along with a relentless drive for self-improvement. Productivity and achievement take the cake as the Achiever's core values. Getting things done is more important than too much planning and "wasted" time spent daydreaming.

How Can I Recognize a Type Three?

With refined tastes and an impressive drive to accomplish more, Achievers are socially adept conversationalists with a talent for beating deadlines and looking crazy-good while doing so. They're poised and intuitively know what to say during any situation. They can make friends with just about anyone. Achievers may have top-notch Instagram feeds, a seemingly perfect life, and the charm to prove it. Males and females often portray an image that aligns very strongly to their gender identity (i.e., masculine or feminine). When asked about their five-year plan or career goals, they typically have a well-thought-out mental map of where they want to be.

What Are Achievers Like under Different Levels of Health?

At healthy levels: Achievers are driven, kind, and willing to lend a helping hand. They can push organizations to new, uncharted territories with talent and ease. With their natural charisma and knack for recognizing the potential for their brilliant ideas, Achievers succeed in the workplace and beyond. They're highly adaptable and can push themselves to inspire others and successfully reap the fruits of their labor and creativity. With their witty sense of humor and goofy side, they learn to take life with ease and prioritize their work-life balance. They're organized, on top of their game, and willing to take constructive feedback.

At average levels: Achievers are busybodies, searching for new goals to accomplish and flashy ways to flaunt their expertise. They're almost always on the go with new projects to finish and people with whom to collaborate. Their looming fear of failure propels them to keep up their momentum and continue working hard. Social media becomes a place for constant comparison and expression, which can lead to excessive self-promotional content or arrogance. Achievers are dead-set on being first place in whatever they put their minds and hearts to— whether that's a career goal or project.

At unhealthy levels: Achievers become extremely jealous and view every interaction in terms of a competition, and so may be prone to one-upping others. They seek approval and reassurance from others—when this is not fulfilled, they begin to despair and shut down. The once-driven go-getter becomes lazy, unfulfilled, and prone to developing low self-esteem. Eventually, an Achiever may choose to reject their sense of self and may develop intense mood swings. Many Achievers report feeling like a "hollow shell" after years of curating an image of who they'd like to be. This feeling can lead to major shifts in their career, relationship, or lifestyle. At their worst, they ruthlessly backstab and destroy others' reputations solely for their own benefit.

Type Four

Fours are defined by their sense of being special and different from other people. They are often creative and present a unique, distinctive persona to the people around them. Fours experience a deep conflict in that they long to connect with others, but they feel that because they are so unusual, very few people are able to truly see them as they are.

Fours fear that they are flawed and are missing out on some basic aspect of happiness to which other people have access. To cope with this fear, they amplify what is different and special about themselves, looking for the niche in which they can truly be appreciated.

Defining Characteristics of the Enneagram Type Four

- Distinctive inner and outer presentation
- Prominent artistic outlet(s)
- Quirky and endearing
- Melancholic expression
- Strong sense of identity
- May feel a sense of emptiness
- Passionate about self-expression

What Are Individualists Like?

Individualists may stand out to others with their unique choice of fashion, unconventional lifestyle, and interests or creative works. Offbeat yet endearing, Individualists have a relentless drive to discover and understand who they truly are, deep down. Creation—not consumption—is the key to their well-being.

They spend a large amount of time reflecting on the past and using experiences and feelings as a springboard for creative musings and new projects. Through a process of continuous exploration of the inner self (both their conscious and unconscious sides), Individualists produce original work that is untouched by the expectations of others.

What Are the Individualist's Core Values?

Authenticity and self-expression are the pinnacle of the Individualist's existence. Their ultimate goal is for the world to recognize and appreciate their wholly unique identity. They strongly believe that their striking difference from others should always be consistent. Succumbing to trends would be considered the ultimate act of self-betrayal.

How Can I Recognize a Type Four?

A Four's primary need is to be unique. Because Fours are constantly striving to secure an authentic identity, they believe the only way to do that is by distinguishing themselves from others. Fours love to stand out from the crowd and establish themselves as unique individuals.

Fours value authenticity above everything. Authenticity, both in themselves and others, is crucial for Enneagram Fours. It's important to them that they always try to put forth an honest and true image of themselves, as well as seek it out in everyday life. When it comes to other people, they value authenticity in them just as much as they do in themselves.

Fours rely on their emotions—a lot. I discovered a few years ago that I rely heavily on my emotions when making decisions, but little did I know that this is actually a tendency of Fours. Feeling our emotions so intensely has its ups and downs (just like our moods), however, because our identity is rooted in our feelings.

Fours care deeply about beauty and art. Fours love to find beauty in ordinary things, as well as in the offbeat and untraditional aspects of life. Their love for originality often shows through their hobbies, clothing, or decor because they love to express themselves in any way they can.

Individualists are offbeat, have a strong sense of self-identity, and pride themselves on being unique. They are often found pursuing some sort of creative outlet such as musical comedy or animation. Their ultimate goal is to accurately present their true selves to the world in order to feel real, healthy, and whole. An Individualist's style and way of life often has notes of openness, suggesting that this person is exploring their own psyche. Thrift stores and flea markets are particularly favorite haunts of Individualists.

When it comes to self-expression, Individualists take their presentation very seriously. They constantly evaluate every decision and its alignment to their personal values.

What Are Individualists Like under Different Levels of Health?

At healthy levels: Individualists create thought-provoking and groundbreaking works of art that shift perspectives toward the greater good. They're recognized as idea synthesizers who can help others rethink what art should be like. Major shifts in art styles and fashion eras are largely due to the out-of-the-box thinking from self-actualized Individualists, since they possess the ability to rework past experiences into new works of art. Highly attuned to their complex well of emotions, Individualists undergo a process of metamorphosis in the cocoon of self-acceptance before fully emerging as a butterfly with wings to soar.

At average levels: Individualists let out their stress via creative outlets and may bond with a community of like-minded people to gain inspiration and support along the way. Emotionally intense and introspective, they're seekers of authenticity, but sometimes at the expense of others' patience and feelings. Self-absorbed and artistically expressive, Individualists maintain their personal mood and inspiration board to piece together the different aspects of themselves and their identity. At average levels, they may become hypersensitive to criticism yet firm to themselves. This circumstance results in them actively seeking praise and flattery. They may also be strongly offended if others try to copy or relate to their experiences.

At unhealthy levels: Individualists become excessively moody, depressed, and fragile. They can develop an extreme tendency to ruminate, which is intrusive to their natural creative energies. In extreme cases, they may lose their grip on reality and resort to sensory coping mechanisms such as alcohol or hallucinogens. Their search for the "missing piece" leads Individualists down a never-ending spiral of dead ends and roundabouts. They can fall into the same ditches and make the same mistakes if they refuse to admit to their self-destructive behaviors and thinking patterns. They're prone to developing the belief that there's something inherently "broken" about them. At the peak of their stress, Individualists may delete their entire presence from the web and isolate themselves from the world.

Type Five

Fives are defined by their desire to conserve their energy and to avoid being drained by engagement with the outside world. They focus on being knowledgeable and competent so that they can be as self-sufficient as possible. They enjoy deepening their understanding of the world and expanding their intellect while minimizing their physical and relationship needs.

Fives fear being overwhelmed by their own needs and the needs of others. To cope with this fear, they withdraw from relationships and maintain a minimalist lifestyle, focusing on the intellectual as an escape from the demands of the world.

Defining Characteristics of the Enneagram Type Five

- Appears lost in thought or absentminded
- Extremely difficult-to-crack inner world
- In-depth knowledge on specific subjects of interest
- Gives insightful, well thought-out responses
- Thinks extensively before speaking
- Has clear boundaries between family, friends, and work
- Withdrawn and extremely independent

What Are Investigators Like?

Investigators are the pioneers of independent and critical thinking. They're inquisitive and curious about the connections between underlying themes and the mysteries of the universe. Usually introverted and analytical, Investigators gather and process information to build and synthesize patterns and ideas. Their work spaces are typically minimalist with the exception of a collection of items pertaining to their core interests. They're also fiercely nonconformist and care little about trends or accepted ways of progressing through the stages of life.

What Are the Investigator's Core Values?

With dreams of working and researching alone in a secluded area for the rest of their lives, Investigators hold freedom and autonomy to extremely high standards. They tend to have little regard for social niceties and customs, and are entranced by the potential of the unknown. Above all, Investigators value independence, freedom, and understanding. During times of uncertainty and confusion, Investigators hold a calm and steady mindset to analyze and figure out the best course of action in the grand scheme of things.

How Can I Recognize a Type Five?

Investigators are often stoic and detached. They're fascinated by the ever-expanding realm of unexplored ideas. They are energized by spending hours of time alone, tinkering with their personal projects, and research. The path to mastery in a particular area is a journey each Investigator readily embarks on. They may appear calm and collected on the surface, but when topics of interest come up in conversation, they transform into a giddy and energetic version of themselves. This sudden gear shift may surprise those who were unaware of the Investigator's hidden passions.

What Are Investigators Like under Different Levels of Health?

At healthy levels: Investigators become thought pioneers in their fields of interest and are generally regarded as integral to the intellectual advancement of society. They see large, complex issues with clarity and precision. Through dedication and genuine curiosity, they're able to catalyze change and advance societal movements. The impossible becomes possible for Investigators, who can bring forth new inventions, systems, and ways of thinking with quiet confidence. They become subject matter experts who freely share their wisdom and discoveries with the public. With a talent for simplifying the complicated, Investigators have the potential to communicate previously mind-boggling topics with radical clarity.

At average levels: Investigators are offbeat, withdrawn, and emotionally closed off. They may have a select few esoteric interests that they hide from the public eye—and opt to present an aloof and distant aura. They're well-versed in topics of their interest and may be named a "bookworm" by peers. During their free time, Investigators tap into the different worlds they've created in their minds to escape from the mundane aspects of everyday life, such as chores or errands. They may delve into their large collection of books, for example, or enjoy playing strategic board or card games for leisure.

At unhealthy levels: Investigators cut off their entire social world and may develop tunnel vision. They begin to have far-off and radical views, losing grip with reality. With a lack of emotional awareness and foresight, Investigators can find themselves in heated disputes with no clear answers. As a result, some friendships may be severed in the process, which would certainly baffle Investigators. They may rationalize that they're better off without the presence of people altogether and choose to escape the real world. In addition, they can become addicted to far-off theories few can wrap their heads around and stubbornly cling to a sense of intellectual superiority. This ultimately drives people even further away. At their worst, Investigators can become misanthropic and bitter.

Type Six

Sixes are defined by their desire for safety and security, and are known as the Loyalists of the Enneagram. They seek to anticipate and avoid risk, and to ally themselves with trustworthy authority figures and institutions. Sixes are alert and vigilant, always thinking several steps ahead to anticipate and prepare for what could go wrong.

Sixes fear being unprepared and unable to defend themselves from danger. To cope with this fear, they attempt to be prepared for every possible turn of events.

Defining Characteristics of the Enneagram Type Six

- Strong identification with a social group
- Organized and well-liked
- Good at managing finances
- Excellent team player
- Belongs to a tight-knit group of friends
- Clear communicators
- Detail-oriented and precise

What Are Loyalists like?

Sixes are dedicated and responsible individuals who are keen on belonging to a social group and finding their fit in the world. They can either be phobic or counter-phobic, which deals with their nervous energy and how it presents itself to the outer world.

Here's how to tell the two apart: phobic Sixes deliberately move away from the source(s) of their fear and tend to fly under the radar. They're open and expressive about their vulnerabilities and weaknesses, so others can understand their situation and line of thought. This is their prime defense mechanism to avoid being manipulated.

The counter-phobic Sixes, on the other hand, possess a high-strung, irrational fear of fear itself—which may paradoxically translate to rule-breaking. They try to keep up an image of independence on the surface: a tough exterior to shield their persistent internal uncertainty.

What Are the Loyalist's Core Values?

Security, commitment, and a sense of connectedness with the group are what drive a Six's actions. They stand strong by the people in their lives who have earned a spot in their hearts. Seeking safety, Loyalists value those who can reassure them of their importance and connection.

Trust is the most important value for Sixes. With all the time they spend thinking up a flurry of hypothetical scenarios, knowing someone has their back is extraordinarily comforting. They seek peace within themselves, although this initially proves to be a challenge. Through trial and error, Sixes slowly build trust and confidence over time to effectively tackle any situation.

How Can I Recognize a Type Six?

Unassuming and tolerant, Sixes blend into the social sphere seamlessly and are always willing to support their loved ones. They're great at keeping secrets and take privacy very seriously. At work, Sixes are the employees that stick around and do overtime with ease to support the organization and keep tasks running smoothly.

Sixes actively seek reassurance for their actions and can smell potential issues from miles away. They probably have accumulated a mental compilation of troubleshooting guides for scenarios experienced in the past. This helps them feel in control of potentially risky situations if they come across any of them again.

What Are Sixes Like under Different Levels of Health?

At healthy levels: Sixes are caring, generous, and thoughtful team players who move colleagues and friends forward in a positive direction. They're valuable and hardworking employees who take great pride in serving an organization and will make every effort to hone their skills. During times of stress, they know how to handle and diffuse the nerves with finesse. They develop secure attachment styles and easily trust others. Through their patience and courage, Sixes can learn to accept their independence and express themselves freely in the world. At their best, Sixes are able to let go of their worries and focus on matters they can change in the present moment.

At average levels: Sixes are mentally acute yet highly skeptical, and seek security and group approval for their actions. They become aware of their shortcomings and their self-esteem may fluctuate from time to time. When there's a disconnect between their position and the group, Sixes become noticeably agitated and nervous. To prevent disappointment, Sixes may mentally prepare themselves with the worst case scenario before carrying out a task. They have a tendency to over-analyze messages or information as it comes in, which further fuels their anxiety—and leads to mixed signals. This confuses others, so the whole thing winds up becoming a vicious cycle of worry.

At unhealthy levels: Sixes become extremely paranoid and suspicious of everything and everyone in their path. They're prone to developing anxiety due to their hypervigilance to any impending (real or imagined) sources of harm. As a result, false memories may form and they may start to suspect others are trying to fool them, when in fact these Sixes have become masters at fooling themselves. When events go out of the frying pan and into the fire, Sixes can develop overwhelming and debilitating anxiety from the illusion of constant danger. This anxiety causes them to psychologically latch and cling onto a protective figure in their lives in order to get through each day (also called codependency). When exasperated and fed up, Sixes will project their insecurities onto others and claim they've done something, when it was all brewed up and imagined from the beginning.

Type Seven

Sevens are defined by their desire to experience everything life has to offer while avoiding pain and boredom. They appear to others to be lively, fun-loving, and hedonistic. Sevens are often very busy people who bounce from one activity to another in their quest to squeeze every possible bit of enjoyment out of life.

Sevens fear getting stuck in a rut and missing out on the good life. More than anything, they want to avoid feeling bored, sad, or uninspired. They cope with this fear by constantly seeking out exciting, novel, and fun experiences.

Defining Characteristics of the Enneagram Type Seven

- Always on the go
- Wide range of interests
- Childlike enthusiasm and energy
- Curious, sparkling eyes
- Many ongoing professional and creative projects
- Upbeat and optimistic; glass-half-full outlook
- Well-liked and popular among peers

What Are Enthusiasts Like?

Wide-eyed and filled to the brim with endless energy, Enthusiasts are the playful and busy optimists of the world. Their relentless curiosity for new information and experiences plays into their (often-impressive) stories and gift of gab. At the end of a workday, their minds are often still buzzing with new ideas to explore. They're charming storytellers with a passion for many different hobbies and see the glass as half-full. Bright and expressive, Enthusiasts see the world as their playground and can be considered the eternal children of the Enneagram.

What Are the Enthusiast's Core Values?

Flexibility, happiness, and novelty. Variety is the Enthusiast's bread (not spice!) of life. Enthusiasts seek out eye-opening experiences and sensations—to take in and see the value and meaning in everything. Open-mindedness paired with a non-judgmental attitude is what makes the Enthusiast tick. They believe each person should be given the chance to explore all they possibly can; to them, each moment has its beauty, as long as you look carefully enough.

How Can I Recognize a Type Seven?

Whimsical and free-spirited, Enthusiasts experience life with bright eyes and an open mind. With an impressively wide and far-reaching collection of talents and interests, they have active imaginations that soar and shine when gifted with new and exciting opportunities. At work, they are highly productive and get along well with others. They tend to climb the corporate ladder fairly easily and become a favorite in the lunchroom. With an infinite number of topics to talk about, their natural charisma draws in even the shyest of individuals. When faced with change, they strut forward with pride and boldly traverse through the unknown.

What Are Enthusiasts Like Under Different Levels of Health?

At healthy levels: Enthusiasts see connections between their areas of interest and expertise, and are able to focus their energy wisely in ventures that benefit something greater than themselves. Through every experience, they can see the lessons learned and be grateful for everything that passes, both the good and the bad. They can manage the method to their madness with finesse and inspire others in the process. Their positive energy is infectious, combined with their curiosity for learning and open-mindedness—it's a triple threat. Better yet, they're able to perfect their work-life balance while still making time to embark on new journeys and keep their personal happiness tanks full.

At average levels: Enthusiasts throw themselves in a slew of constant activity and constantly seek the next high. They're fun, busy, and all-around spontaneous individuals. They combat their stress with a growing list of fun projects to undertake. They're adrenaline junkies whose habits may spiral into serious addictions if this scattered energy is mismanaged. Future-oriented and almost always excited for something, Enthusiasts rewrite their lives to maximize happiness and minimize or even deny pain. To do so, they plunge head-first into various forms of escapism: everything from reading, movies, exercise and romance, to alcohol, psychedelics and the like.

At unhealthy levels: Enthusiasts become burnt out, cynical, and overly critical of the seemingly illogical systems that surround them. Minute issues with others become highly irritating and everything suddenly becomes a nuisance. They may also become overwhelmingly narcissistic in their actions and presentation, and come off as flashy. In the worst case, Enthusiasts begin to feel like they'll never fully understand what they're truly seeking out of life. Jumping from place to place or person to person, Enthusiasts lose a sense of groundedness and may appear to live in a perpetual fantasy world instead of reality. When they realize the made-up world is only an illusion, they lose control over their mood and tumble into extreme emotional highs and lows.

Type Eight

Eights are defined by their desire to be powerful and to avoid any vulnerability. They present a confident, assertive, and decisive image to others. Eights can be argumentative and intimidating; it is important to them to stand up for what they believe in and to protect those who are weaker than themselves.

Eights fear being vulnerable and powerless more than anything, and cope with this fear by always being strong and in control.

Defining Characteristics of the Enneagram Type Eight

- Independent and self-sufficient
- A fierce and certain look
- Determination and stamina
- Very energetic and busy
- Fiery passions and power
- Stubborn and headstrong
- Serious about control over their environment

What Are Challengers Like?

Goal-oriented and self-competent, Challengers trailblaze boldly through all walks of life and take great pride in their independence and sharp minds. They hold their heads up high and will pick themselves right back up after each stumble—stronger than before. As children, they may have been called "bossy" by peers. They typically take charge during group projects or meetings and find themselves at ease in leadership positions. The opinions of others will have absolutely no effect on their position on an issue, as they pride themselves on being fully capable and self-sufficient.

What Are the Challenger's Core Values?

Competence, influence, power, and control—Challengers crave respect as opposed to status or being liked by the group. Challengers are set to make an impact and won't back down. They pride themselves on their strength, honesty, and truthfulness. Challengers also possess an extremely strong inner sense of justice. Loyalty also plays a major role in Challengers' value system. They're devoted to those who have proven themselves over time and will stand by them until the end—through hell and high water. When danger comes and their loved ones are in trouble, the Challenger will confidently stretch their wings to protect them.

How can I recognize a Type Eight?

Naturally accustomed to leadership roles, the Challenger makes their presence known and carries an aura of confidence and self-assuredness in their speech and walk. They typically believe in the mantra of creating your own luck and work very hard to make things happen, no questions asked. Challengers are ruthlessly independent and are unafraid of confrontation, which can get them into major trouble at times. They naturally butt heads with authority, especially when met with the classic, "You must do this, because I told you so." Respect is earned through reason and competency, and not through age or status.

What Are Challengers Like under Different Levels of Health?

At healthy levels: Challengers can be a champion of ideas for those who are oppressed. They're strong and confident leaders who can be the backbone and driving force for causes and communities. Their energy and commitment to improve upon society and themselves blossoms into new gardens where Challengers can sow their seeds with care. To close friends and family members, Challengers are generous and intensely loving individuals who freely offer refuge and advice. When they learn to develop their caring side, gratitude and joy emerges from their core selves. With this newfound sense of tenderness, Challengers become aware of others' needs and will freely drop their tough persona.

At average levels: Challengers are competitive and may view friendships or business relations as a battlefield, always looking for the next challenge to win. They're assertive and stubborn, but also self-confident and competent. During their downtime, they critically evaluate their actions and work toward self-improvement. They avoid showing vulnerability, which can be a roadblock to connection and intimacy. Doing so would demonstrate weakness, which is absolutely unacceptable in their books. As a result, they can be seen as highly ambitious yet intimidating by peers. Their confidence and stamina lift them to new heights, with each failure serving as a kick for more effort.

At unhealthy levels: Challengers can become tyrannical and intimidating, scaring others off at first glance. They become addicted to the pursuit of power and will destroy anything blocking their way with fury. The feelings and emotions of others become insignificant, as they become blindfolded to the softer side of the human psyche. When their delusions of power get out of hand, Challengers become stone-cold and take an antagonistic stand to anyone who dares to question them and their motives. They may use empty threats to regain power over others and turn existing relationships into tests—where one can only pass or fail. Others may turn their backs on Challengers, who will reason that they were better off working alone. In the end, they may force themselves into loneliness.

Type Nine

Nines are defined by their desire to maintain a sense of inner peace and harmony, and to avoid conflict or other emotional disturbances. They are typically agreeable, calm, and easy to be around. Nines rarely rock the boat, but they can be stubborn. While they typically go with the flow, they dislike being controlled and will respond with passive resistance if pushed too far.

Nines fear being too needy and, as a result, pushing people away. They cope with this fear by submitting to the desires and agendas of the people around them. They act agreeable in order to be included.

Defining Characteristics of the Enneagram Type Nine

- Calm, collected demeanor

- Ability to diffuse conflict with ease
- Zen-like presence
- Mellow and soothing voice
- Wide circle of acquaintances
- Generally liked by most people
- Fluid, slow movements and gestures

What Are Peacemakers Like?

Gentle and agreeable, Peacemakers are the skilled mediators and counselors in a group of friends or coworkers. They work hard behind the scenes in order to keep the group harmony steady and flowing. As children, they knew how to get along with each classmate, making them a great addition to any group project. They can easily see the many different sides to an issue and tend not to jump to conclusions quickly, if at all. Complacent and humble, Peacemakers are stable and gentle, willing to go the extra mile to avoid rocking the boat. They're appreciative of the little things others do and the simple pleasures in life.

What Are the Peacemaker's Core Values?

Harmony, kindness, and unity with the world. Idealistic and well-wishing, Peacemakers aim to be the glue that holds the entire group together—whether they're with family, friends or colleagues. The quickest way into a Peacemaker's heart is to acknowledge their contributions and reassure them of their importance. Gently sharing their nuggets of wisdom and serenity with others, Peacemakers believe in the power of forgiveness and acceptance. External comfort paired with a sense of inner balance make up the Peacemakers' ideal lifestyle—and they gladly create this atmosphere through every aspect of their lives.

How Can I Recognize a Type Nine?

Peacemakers are social chameleons who can adapt to the group dynamic easily and help others get along. They're soft-spoken yet loyal and fun to be around, intuitively knowing how to include and engage everyone in conversation. Peacemakers are cooperative and always willing to let someone join the circle and state their own opinions. Despite being firm in their personal stances, they make an effort to neutralize tension and restore group harmony. Easygoing and willing to tolerate everyone, Peacemakers retain their self-esteem through being kind and helpful to others. They enjoy the comfortable side of life and may have a personal space to recharge from the outer world. Many are deep seekers of meaning and have a fond appreciation of spirituality and a sense of connectedness with the universe.

What Are Peacemakers Like under Different Levels of Health?

At healthy levels: Peacemakers use their natural conflict-diffusing powers to maintain harmony and bring on the social fluidity in a group. They're natural counselors and teachers with a gift for persuasion and mediation. Optimistic and fully alive, they have a strong self-identity and can ascribe to a simple and healthy lifestyle. When self-actualized, Peacemakers can develop a keen sense of ambition and take the necessary steps to use their calm energy to better others' lives and well-being. They're excellent communicators and are patient enough to deal with any situation. Self-actualized Peacemakers can use their deep well of wisdom to help others resolve their internal and external conflicts.

At average levels: Peacemakers stay out of the limelight and maintain regular contact with their close friends and acquaintances. They may have issues with procrastination and can often correct their work habits with consistent schedules and careful planning. For Peacemakers, this is an important lifelong process. Peacemakers are change-adverse and lovers of the comfy and familiar. They enjoy the idea of a cozy retreat to take a break from the world and simply relax. They have the tendency to avoid direct confrontation and run away from problems when they emerge.

At unhealthy levels: Peacemakers become lethargic, unable to concentrate on a task and believe they do not matter in the grand scheme of things. They may become sluggish and unable to focus, simply procrastinating time away instead of achieving anything. Cruising through life on autopilot, Peacemakers go through the motions without trying to set goals or make improvements. On another note, Peacemakers may become internally self-critical for not being able to carry through with plans and establish a firm identity. Extremely stressed Peacemakers often fail to set personal boundaries, which may lead to burnout and emotional exhaustion. Their passive-aggressiveness ends up straining existing relationships.

The Enneagram and Stress Patterns

Dearest Reader,

Life, they say, is not all a bed of roses. In all your endeavors, you could be faced with lots of challenges and setbacks.

Have you ever been so stressed that you literally "flipped a switch" and acted out, causing people to remark that you were acting like someone else? Maybe you felt like you had an out-of-body experience, or you felt completely beyond your own control and as though you had demons in you.

Well, no need to panic, because according to the Enneagram system, there's a reason for that! Each type has an area of disintegration (known as stress) that it falls into. When all the types become especially stressed, they become disillusioned and may exhibit ugly traits antithetical to their status quo. It is also important to note that before this happens, there must also be a sequence of unhealthy behaviors or feelings that may occur—which are called Factors.

This whole process is what I earlier termed in the introduction as "Tunnel Vision." This book will give you a comprehensive view on what triggers stress (Factors), the aftermath and effects, and how to contain this surge. In truth, stress is not a curse—it is bound to happen, but if we don't control our stress deferment, it could distort our mental grasp of our personality.

Join me as we explore an in-depth view of what stress is. Keep scrolling and read deeply.

What Is Stress in the Enneagram?

Stress in the Enneagram is an abrupt deferment in an individual's attitude owning to some unhealthy behaviors or unconducive environment that they are introduced to. It is also seen as the disintegration from someone's behavior and characteristics, leading to strains in their dealings with their fellow mates.

One thing you must know about stress is that it is inevitable; it happens whenever the going gets tough. Although everyone differs in how they respond to stress, different types of anxiety affects different numbers in different ways. For instance, a Nine handles stress very differently than an Eight.

Here are the salient stress factors each Enneagram type personality experiences and their effects on the types.

Enclosed below is a guide.

The Stressed Enneagram One (The Reformer/Perfectionist)

What stresses out the Enneagram One and how do they respond to it?

Factors

Being a die-hard perfectionist around lazy people or people you cannot count on or depend on when things goes sour.

The following phrase could have been coined for Ones: "Don't sell me dreams; sell me ideas." Not seeing any action being taken toward a specific goal or ambition can make Ones relapse and become laidback. This relapse, in turn, creates stress for the One.

Unfortunately, Ones are pretty bad at handling failure. Being perfectionists, their mentality is always geared toward winning, and so when failure occurs, they cannot handle the shame or disgrace they feel over the mistakes they've made.

Being taken for granted: One thing a perfectionist cherishes is respect. They believe it is reciprocal as they strive to be of good conduct. However, when taken for granted, they tend to question themselves for being in that situation in the first place.

Falling Short of Expectations: This is also another factor that could lead to stress in a One. Every One has their own standards and not living up to their own expectations is fatal for their mental health.

If there's anything that pisses off Ones, it's others not living up to their expectations—I know you're probably about to remark that Ones are a bit judgemental. That's not even the underlying issue— equipped with a high set of uncompromising moral standards, this set of people views life events in the order of right or wrong, according to their internal mental default settings.

Unfortunately, this mindset does not give any room for anything in between right or wrong (that is, you are either for them or against them). Needless to say, Ones are great enforcers (hammers) as they won't stop unless their plans have been achieved.

This bossiness might seem like the majority of a One's stress is inflicted on those around them; however, they have an inward voice that forces them to be the responsible one while others are slacking.

Corruption in the world: All Ones ever want is a sane world where good reigns, and bad is thwarted and punished.

Hypocrisy: "The only vice that cannot be forgiven is Hypocrisy. The repentance of a hypocrite is itself hypocrisy." – William Hazlitt (1778-1830)

As said earlier, Ones are people of unflinching integrity. It's either the easier wrong or the harder right. The most unusual thing ever observed in a One may be their "0.01% empathy" geared toward the opposite side of their ideas, save for a hypocrite. Hypocrisy means a lot to Ones; if you are never a person of your words, dubious and overwhelmingly selfish, you've just gotten yourself a lifelong enemy in a One.

Apathy: The source of a One's apathy tends to come from a lack of conformity to their environment, or the working decisions or mechanisms done in such a place (be it work, relationships, goal-setting, etc.). This noncomformity is usually because this place doesn't tally with their principles. So in order to let peace reign, Ones decide to be either laidback or disconnected from such activity.

Punctuality: One of the perks that come with self-discipline is punctuality. Showing up late to a meeting or appointment that they are heading will pose a personal problem for them.

Messy surroundings: Name the first thing you think of that might be distasteful to a perfectionist and you'll come up with dirtiness first. You will see Ones burning up when you make a mess, forget to flush the toilet, or leave food crumbs on the kitchen table. They even struggle with a disorganized room or schedule, etc. All these things piss them off big time!

Aftermath/Effects

Normally, Reformers are said to be conservative and pragmatic. Once under stress, however, they suddenly become moody and withdrawn. In their quest to live up to the ever-increasing standards they set for themselves, they grow weary in most cases, and this exhaustion leads to deep resentment and anger. However, because they are always trying to preserve their dignity and respect, they repress their anger and it somehow manages to leak out in various ways—for example, snappish or irritated comments, cynical jokes, or sarcastic jabs. If their stress is at its height, Ones may lose their usual self-discipline and become hostile, withdrawn, and emotionally reactive. They might overreact, break some of their own rules, or try to be reckless. At this point, it may be as though they have killed the self-criticism inside them, and, for the moment, are letting loose that demon/rebel that was always hiding in the corner. Overall, they may become more self-indulgent, self-conscious, and dramatic.

How to Help a One Who Is Experiencing Stress:

- Whenever they have an outburst, let them be. You must never be judgmental toward them.
- Take on some of the responsibilities around them without having to be asked.
- Acknowledge the effort, hard work, and dedication they've put forth on a goal. Be grateful and appreciative for all the things they've done for you. Negativity is the last thing Ones want to be around when they're stressed.
- Give them some time and space all alone to come back to their senses.
- Understand that in this condition, they might be especially moody and critical. So be patient and employ empathy in your communication with them.
- Never try to analyze their blame shifting as it makes them feel judgemental of themselves. Rather, let them know that even if they have superpowers, that doesn't mean they are responsible for everything.
- Try to temporarily divest them of some of their responsibilities. A break is what they truly deserve!
- Clean and tidy up the house or the area they're in. Give them that assuring sense that things are in order.

- Constantly remind them of the fact that nobody is perfect and if they're being self-critical all the time, they are prone to making lots of mistakes.

- After their anger has subsided, engage them in recreation or give them something safe to play with. Watch a comedy with them, take a walk with them outside, or try to make them laugh.

The Stressed Enneagram Two (The Giver/Helper)

The Giver is always a type whom everyone wants in their life. The Two is a selfless character and helper that won't mind going without just to make another comfortable. However, it is shocking to see that this type can also get stressed, which shows you that this world is never balanced. So what stresses a Two?

Factors

Lonely days/nights: Inside their heart, a Two wants to give their all to further a goal. You may think they'd make friends for that—but no, they stay lonely and here's why: try putting them in a situation where they have nothing left to give and watch their supposed friends disappear!. A Two can feel it—they know they aren't actually valued by some people whom they call friends, but they can't do anything about it because they are just so fulfilled by helping others.

Being taken for granted: Because a giver is so engrossed in helping others, people tend to take this rare trait for weakness. Therefore, Twos are taken for granted and sometimes disrespected if they feel too overwhelmed with duties/responsibilities to help someone who has grown accustomed to relying on them. It is common with this type of personality to hear them saying things like, "I've been lending James money since last year. But today, I couldn't lend him any because I'm broke, and guess what? He started yelling at me!"

Saying "yes" to too many things and burning themselves out: A Two personality finds nothing in this world harder to say than "no." A Two may feel that they're letting you down if they say no to you, but it's an utterly unrealistic way of living. They can easily find themselves stretched out of resources or funds or time, or simply out of physical energy to cater to others. Yet, they still try! And the mere fact that they never say no means that some people don't realize or care how hard things have become for them. As a result, people tend to not only misunderstand them, but also take them for granted.

Not getting affirmation or gratitude for their kind deeds: Inasmuch as they extend their generosity beyond their bounds, people still tend to take Twos for granted and will not even thank them for their actions. Although many people castigate this type of personality as being weak and gullible, a Two's use of selective generosity helps gather much love and followers. It may sound too desperate, but the sad reality is that a naturally kind person is often never valued among their peers.

Being around emotionally distant people: Despite all the care and thoughtfulness they lavish on their friends, Twos are not always rewarded by having good relationships with people. Sometimes they attract people who aren't so nice or who are emotionally distant. There are plenty of insensitive people out there and plenty of people looking for someone to use, and Twos can often attract them or find themselves targeted by them.

Not having their kindness reciprocated: At this point, you should know that with a Two in your life, your problem becomes their problem because they try to attend to their needs by helping you. But the question is: can you consistently reciprocate this gesture? Your failure to do so creates both physical and mental stress for Twos. On the physical side, they end up sacrificing their own time, efforts, needs, and desires until they run short of energy. On the mental side, they not only become drained but feel used by others and experience depression over it.

Aftermath/Effects

The main desire of a Two is to feel loved for who they truly are. The phrase "true love" is more than a literary device to them, as these types need to nurture themselves as much as they do others. However, they often overextend themselves on other people's behalf, to the point that they may come across as imposing, with the hope that through their selfless pursuits, they will earn a sense of worth and love.

When these types are severely stressed, they tend to become more blunt and aggressive. Usually noted for being kind-hearted and gentle, they suddenly exhibit shocking inner demons. They will confront people directly for their misdeeds, say words directly to anyone without minding the content, and won't hold back in arguing about matters that they'd normally avoid talking about. This directness is usually shocking at first to people who are used to the Two's normal gregarious, warm, friendly, and empathetic attitude. As a result this personality type tends to go extreme in being more concerned with their own survival (even if it's at others' detriment). They'll work harder to exert more power and control over the world around them.

How to Help a Two Who Is Experiencing Stress:

- Be grateful and always acknowledge everything that they have done. In doing so, you sublimely show them that you care about them.

- In order to prevent them from overstepping their limits while extending care to others, help them draft and set healthy limits to guide their actions.

- Although setting these limits may make them feel bad or even guilty, it is pertinent to constantly remind them of the need to not worry so much about what other people think of them. Also, remind them to be pickier over who should be part of their lives. For instance, they need to define who their loyal friends and loved ones truly are before they go to the trouble of helping them.

- Try enlightening them on the dangers of pleasing everyone. Get them to understand that in this life, one's decisions cannot favor everyone and that it's okay to not be perfect.

- As also applies to Ones, do not be judgmental of Twos, as it may cause them to resent you. Twos will react with more aggression than usual when they are stressed. Understand that this aggression is temporary and try not to judge too harshly unless they are endangering someone.

- Give them freedom if they want to vent, write down their feelings, or listen to a particular song (preferably not a moody song) to find a mirror for their feelings.

- Help them explore their creative modes of self-expression through yoga, drawing, singing, or writing.

- Tell them that although it's true that "we rise by raising others", it's still not selfish for them to take care of themselves and spend time on their own pursuits.

- Help them in their day-to-day schedules. Help them plan their days as well as drafting and cancelling some of their non-essential obligations so they can get a little time to themselves.

The Stressed Enneagram Three (The Achiever)

Highly focused and competitive, Threes frequently burn out to make the most of everything they do. Not afraid of a challenge, they enjoy proving themselves and standing out amid a crowd of mediocre individuals. This type of personality is known to be a high achiever, but their success can come with a lot of struggle. However, when Threes are highly stressed, they can push themselves way too hard and punish themselves too viciously for their failures.

So what stresses out Enneagram Threes?

Factors

Feeling like a failure: There is nothing more destructive to the successful dreams of a Three than the feeling of failure. It is not true that this type cannot overcome failure with hindsight—after all, they are resilient achievers. The problem starts when they nurture thoughts of hopelessness.

Feeling incompetent or being around incompetence: Because a Three wants to be successful and several steps ahead of everyone, including both their peer group and competitors, they will do anything to achieve this feat. However, when they fall short, they tend to withdraw and bow out shamefully. This is similar to how they relate to and treat others who fall short of their standards.

Not being acknowledged for what they do: There's a secret that lies within the lives of the Threes: they care less about self-validation than they do about validation from others. They're constantly working hard to keep up appearances and to be looked up to. One thing they hate bitterly is either being ignored or not being acknowledged for what they do or are doing.

Not accomplishing things: A Three is meant to strive and prosper through thick and thin, no matter the odds. Therefore, Threes find it demoralizing when their efforts to accomplish certain tasks or goals are not yielding fruit. This lack of accomplishment can affect them badly.

Losing: "We can do it. Yes, we can!" – Barack Obama

This quote is emblematic of a Three. However, what Threes don't seem to understand is how to handle failure. In fact, the act of losing infuriates them. A Three would rather ditch their cards than lose the whole hand, and this fact may threaten their personal relationships with people plus their mental drive for their aspirations.

Comparing themselves to others who are highly successful: "Stay in your own lane" is a phrase that a Three would do well to internalize (as hard as it is for a Three). This type is so competitive that everything they do, all on the basis of being ahead of everyone, even if being ahead is to their detriment. At this point, they lose focus on who they are and mistakenly look to set the standard of being better than other people and more successful. They find it hard to realize that everyone has a different path or lane to achieving success.

Feeling worthless or undesirable: The feeling of uselessness comes in two ways: first, a Three may unduly "ditch" other people whom they feel they have no use for. Also, on the other side of the fence, a Three may feel ditched by others and that's where the problem arises. If a Three feels useless, their confidence is dealt a heavy blow, which will trigger their stress mode.

Not being challenged: As said earlier, Threes are highly ambitious, adventurous, and will stand up to any challenges they face. But just like an engine that has not been oiled for years, they can become rusty with their behavior and thereby exhibit stressful attitudes.

Being around people who lack vision: The life of a Three is driven by the motivation to strive for success. This has to be achieved over a range of aspects, especially friends, peers, and family or within their inner circle of business. If the people around Threes are lackluster to them, you will probably see a full display of stressful behaviors from the Three.

Aftermath/Effects

When extreme stress hits Threes, they can suddenly flip a switch and become more listless and apathetic. They fill their time with busywork to try to avoid facing the reality of the problems they're dealing with. Instead of actually doing anything, they may get caught up in fantasies of their next big success. They also may feel more sensitive than usual, but will avoid facing their feelings directly. These stress episodes are confusing for them and their loved ones because Threes are typically so hard-working and ambitious.

How to Help a Three Who Is Experiencing Stress:

- Let them take off their mask of competence and capability. Patiently let them talk about what's bothering them or give them time alone to decompress.

- Help them take deep breaths and tune into their body. Are they hungry? Thirsty? Tired? In pain? Help them recognize their physical needs.

- Encourage them (non-forcefully) to talk about their feelings. Remind them that you're there to listen, not to judge. Give them a safe space to express their vulnerabilities without judging, offering advice, or coddling them. Simply listen.

- Be authentic about your own vulnerabilities. This will help them to feel safe being vulnerable with you.

- Draw their attention toward a creative avenue. Creative activity often helps Threes tremendously. Give them time to write, draw, listen to music, etc.

- Acknowledge their successes and how they've helped you.

- Try to clean any messes in their surroundings. Disordered external surroundings tend to stress them out more.

The Stressed Enneagram Four (The Individualist/Romantic)

Often filled with a sense of longing, romance, and melancholy, Fours are good at communicating with the world through their emotions. They're amazing at empathizing with other people using their personal experiences. They are also full-time idealists who believe in good relationships and growth, and they enjoy living with an open heart. But when problems hindering this vision arises, how do Fours respond?

Factors

Going along with the crowd: Even if they try to connect with the world, a Four wants to be profoundly unique in everything they do. They hate living under a conservative system where a single standard applies to all. Therefore, the very idea of going along with the crowd is already self-defeating to them before this idea manifests in reality.

Too many external pressures: Living a stress-free life is a major goal of a Four. The emotions of a Four could serve them wrong, however, as they tend to burst when faced with lots of pressure.

Feeling misunderstood or criticized: If doing the best for everyone were a crime, Fours would be guilty and serving a life sentence. Fours are genuinely expressive in both their actions and thoughts. The problem lies in that they cannot handle criticism nor are they good at handling their actions or concepts being misunderstood.

Being micro-managed: Expecting low standards of Fours? Don't do it! Being micro-managed or under-managed is a drastic turnoff to a Four and will negatively affect a Four's behavior. They tend to feel hard done by and underestimated, anxious about not realizing their full potential; hence, the dramatic change in their behavior when being micro-managed.

Less progress on their creative goals: Creativity is in the very soul of a Romantic. Many Fours are notable for excelling in areas such as poetry, art, music, etc. Therefore, feeling creatively blocked is a huge detriment to a Four. They can't handle it because it's the only way they can connect with others.

Struggling emotionally: Struggling emotionally is a huge deficit in the life of a Four. The loss of people close to them or non-reciprocated love from people they've showered with affection could lead to an emotional breakdown. A huge problem presents itself for them when they cannot fake it out with a smiling face. If they are sad, they are sad.

Having their feelings dismissed: Being expressive, a Four will always tell you how they feel. The problem comes when you choose to ignore or dismiss their feelings. Fours tend to get pissed off when you do this because they feel rejected.

Living in dull, non-personalized surroundings: Being creative and expressive entails staying in an environment where one can grasp and relate with everything in the environment. To a Four, this is the starting point of their awakening. If the surroundings present a bad scenario, their energy drains and their expressions become vividly negative. But if the environment and the people are appealing to them, the case is reversed.

Aftermath/Effects

Being authentic and imaginative is vital to a Four. When these characteristics are under threat, melancholia sets in, making the Fours fail to establish their revered belief in being deeply authentic and finding their unique identity in the world. They hate feeling forced into a box or unable to express their true feelings and ideals. When stressed, Fours tend to isolate themselves and brood over their negative feelings. They dwell on the darkness of their emotions and allow those feelings to engulf them. If stress increases to an extreme level, they may suddenly change and become more outgoing and anxious for human interaction. They might try too hard to please others or find ways to get closer to people. They will seem more needy, expressive, and people-pleasing. They'll crave affirmation and will be terrified of being abandoned or rejected. They will try to help others in order to regain a sense of being needed by the ones they love.

How to Help a Four Who Is Experiencing Stress:

- Allow them to express their feelings. Don't tell them how they feel or cut them off. Understand that their feelings are unique to them.
- Remind them of what's real and what they can count on. Don't minimize their feelings, but point out the reality of the situation while empathizing with them.
- Remind them of their talents and strengths.
- Help them set up some positive routines that will create a more peaceful atmosphere in their home.
- Set up healthy boundaries if they are regularly using you as an emotional dumping ground.
- Remind them of what's positive in the present moment.
- Offer empathy before advice.
- Let them know that they are lovable regardless of how different they are from others.

The Stressed Enneagram Five

Profoundly known as the Observer, this personality type consists of the quiet, observant people of the Enneagram group. Fives prefer secrecy to expression. Because they observe a lot, they are highly objective, as they devote their time researching problems as thoroughly and extensively as possible before implementing solutions. While this type may perceive their path to development being one of learning and expanding their awareness, their relationships with friends and family can sometimes drift widely. The problem of withdrawing or withholding from people is one of the factors that triggers their stress pattern. So what are the others?

Factors

Lack of privacy: One thing a Five loves is "me time." Their privacy is something they would never trade anything for. A lack of privacy or being intruded on could trigger their stress pattern.

Feeling incompetent or incapable: Because they can struggle with relating to people, Fives often tend to be ostracized or left out of the action. This, in turn, detrimentally affects them as they feel they are being left out due to their incompetence or incapability of handling specific tasks.

Feeling of detachment: In a bid to escape emotional pressure, fear, anxiety, and other stress-related problems, Fives tend to withdraw from people, which may at first guarantee them personal freedom, but in the long run, may detach them from the physical world. Everything they do, act, wear, or relate to may be deemed "weird" by their fellow humans.

Physical malnutrition and neglect: Fives pursue intellectual knowledge and analysis. As such, they may spend their time consuming books, theses, and empirical research without catering to their physical needs and health. In some cases, they could starve themselves while focusing on their intellectual pursuits.

Being overwhelmed by fears and dark thoughts: Because Fives think and observe so much, their thoughts are often overwhelmed by fears, anxiety, and a deep resentfulness of things not seen. In addition, they may find it hard giving out information and mostly withhold their knowledge.

Feeling like life is meaningless: When consumed with the fear of the unknown, Fives are unfazed by life. Most of the time, you'll find them nonchalant about the things going on around them. The truth is, however, that they are trying hard to escape reality, which we all know is almost impossible.

Loneliness: At the end of the day, Fives experience more loneliness than any other other Enneagram personality. They tend to drift away from the world of people and this negatively impacts their wellness.

Aftermath/Effects

Fives want to master something that separates them from others. These interests often started young, and as they grew up in their homes, they were sometimes misunderstood. They were concerned that they could not handle whatever life threw at them and hoped to feel competent by the mastery of a niche field. Nevertheless, many Fives constantly seek out mastery and understanding, only to lose themselves in the real-world experience of theoretical study. They may become solitary, withdrawn, and nervous over time. Stress builds as they feel their increasing isolation from reality and their own physical self. They try to hide from the entire world amid daily stress and concentrate on their niche interest. The more their tension builds, the more distracted they become. They can drink too much and binge-eat, or go to parties, clubs, and bars to relieve tension. In these moments, they can appear extremely violent and insensitive.

How to Help a Five Who Is Experiencing Stress:

- Help them quiet their mind. Guide them through deep breathing and help them relax their body.

- Help them tune into their body. Are they exhausted? Dehydrated? Hungry? In pain? Fives often detach from their physical needs under stress. Help guide them back to their bodies so that they can get physical peace.

- Get them involved in a healthy activity. Take a walk, jump on a trampoline, go to the zoo, or practice martial arts. These activities can reduce their stress tremendously.

- Remind them that you'll be there for them regardless of whatever happens. Let them know that it's okay for them to tell you about their needs and that it doesn't make them "weak."

- Recognize their accomplishments and unique abilities.
- Help them put their knowledge to the test in the real world when they're feeling less stressed. The more they actualize their abilities, the happier they will become.
- Let them feel their grief. Show that you are trustworthy. Don't coddle them or overly sympathize with them. Just show that you are there for them and remind them not to swallow their feelings. Encourage them to express themselves so that they can find relief.
- Respect their need for privacy.
- Don't interrupt them or barge in on them.

The Stressed Enneagram Six (The Loyalist/Skeptic)

Sixes are hard-working and committed to protection, service, and structure. They want to know what will happen and when it will happen. For instance, they already have a natural disaster plan for worst-case situations and are alert to future disasters. So what stresses out Enneagram Sixes?

Factors

- Undependable people
- Disorder in their environment
- Corruption or chaos in the world
- Not trusting themselves
- Not having a sense of community or support
- Getting lost in catastrophizing

- Feeling unsafe
- Lack of structure or clarity
- Burnout from over-committing and taking on too many responsibilities
- Not finding answers to their questions
- Wishy-washy behavior
- Having other people decide for them
- Feeling distrustful of people close to them
- Making mistakes

Aftermath/Effects

Under stress, Sixes become hyper-aware of all that could go wrong. They become exceedingly anxious and envision horrific possibilities at every turn. They get lost in endless thoughts and negative possibilities, and may get caught up in researching solutions or news stories that might provide answers. They may also seek authority or guidance to help them find the best way to handle the situation. If their stress builds to extreme levels, they disintegrate in the same way a Three does. That is, Sixes become more image-conscious and focused on how they appear to others. They may put on a persona of professionalism and confidence, even becoming boastful and self-promoting. Their work absorbs them and they become fixated on achievement. By being competitive and ambitious, they hope they can assuage their low self-esteem and brutal anxiety.

How to Help a Six Who Is Experiencing Stress:

- Remind them of what's real and dependable.
- Ask them to assume the worst happens. Then what will they do? Letting them talk it out can help them calm down and realistically assess the situation.
- Remind them that the worst could happen, but that the best could happen as well.
- Don't patronize their fears.
- Follow through on your commitments and promises.
- Remind them that you're there for them.
- Help them tune into their body. Guide them through deep breathing.
- Ask them to assess their physical needs. Are they hungry? Tired? Thirsty? Remind them not to forget their physical needs.
- Exercise with them or go for a walk. This can increase stress-reducing endorphins in the brain.
- Help them calm the flurry of internal voices in their mind. Encourage them to listen to their heart and instincts.
- Make sure they're getting time alone.
- Help them cancel non-essential responsibilities that are overwhelming them.

The Stressed Enneagram Seven (The Enthusiast/Adventurer)

Sevens are forward-looking thinkers. They typically follow a constructive and ambitious approach to all their activities and show an interest in many different subjects. They don't want to do only one thing—

instead, they want to preserve their choices and options.

So what stresses out Enneagram Sevens?

Factors

- Being micro-managed
- Not having enough personal freedom
- Lack of free, unstructured time
- Excessive responsibilities
- Being cooped up for too long
- Being stuck in one place for too long
- Boredom
- Doing nitty-gritty, detailed work
- Financial problems
- Being stuck in a routine
- Lack of loyal friendships

Aftermath/Effects

When Sevens are anxious, they become more impulsive and desperate to escape. They can start focusing on pleasant activities and experiences, and become more hedonistic or dispersed than normal. As stress rises to extreme degrees, they may show signs of a One under stress. They limit their typically free-spirited conduct when this happens. They can become hard to live with as they judge people more. In severe cases, they can also scold, pick, or act rudely towards others—seeing all their faults in other people's shortcomings.

How to Help a Seven Who Is Experiencing Stress:

- Help them calm down by taking deep breaths.
- Guide them through observing their feelings, both physical and emotional. They may dislike this initially and need some time alone first. It's important for them to do this though, either alone or with someone they can trust.
- Meditation can be very helpful for Sevens. Encourage them to stick with this, even if it seems boring.
- Encourage them to accept pain as well as pleasure. Help them to realize that pain is an integral part of life and will help them grow.
- Be supportive as they vent or try to deal with their grief.
- Give them delicious, healthy snacks to enjoy.
- Help them to find a song that mirrors their emotions and listen to it with them.

The Stressed Enneagram Eight (The Challenger/Protector)

Eights pursue independence and a sense of power in their world. They are charismatic and devoted. They need freedom, and any situation that eliminates the chances of this will cause tremendous stress and be a major roadblock to their well-being.

So what stresses out Enneagram Eights?

Factors

- Feeling out of control
- Being micro-managed
- Having to be a follower
- Having their autonomy infringed upon

- Not seeing progress toward a goal
- Failure
- Wishy-washy, vapid people
- Manipulative people
- Having to sugarcoat things
- Having to play it safe
- Being around corruption
- Not being challenged

Aftermath/Effects

During stress, Eights can become more confrontational than usual and work harder, trying to achieve more independence and control in their lives. If stress builds to extreme degrees, Eights can suddenly become reclusive and withdrawn. They get stuck in analysis, reading, and information-gathering, trying to find subjects to master in an attempt to feel competent again. They may stop taking care of themselves physically, and become more quiet and detached than usual.

How to Help an Eight Who Is Experiencing Stress:

- Prove that you are someone they can trust. Follow through on your promises and mean what you say.
- Give them some time to themselves to decompress and sort things out.
- Help them tune into their breathing and calm their body.

- Remind them that it's okay to let down their guard around you. Let them know this doesn't make them "weak."
- Let them know if they are intimidating you.
- Show them that progress is being made toward a goal.
- Be clear and direct with them, yet understanding.

The Stressed Enneagram Nine (The Peacemaker/Mediator)

Nines crave inner harmony and peace. They want time to themselves to imagine, contemplate, and explore. They enjoy peaceful, harmonious environments and freedom.

So what stresses out Enneagram Nines?

Factors

- Conflict in their environment
- Being with people who are making a "scene"
- Being forced into a position
- Being ignored or passed over
- Saying "yes" to things they don't want to do
- Dealing with peer pressure
- Losing relationships that are important to them
- Suppressing anger for too long
- Having too many demands on their time

Aftermath/Effects

Nines try to play down their options and requirements during stress to build inner and outer tranquility. They worry about causing more tension inside and outside by affirming themselves. They attempt to contain their rage and fear that it will somehow break them up or kill them. Nines concentrate on building relationships and well-being if tension rises to high levels. They are worried about worst-case situations, and so become gloomy and paranoid. They may blame others for their problems or complain about others' long-suffering. Their typically serene nature breaks down to show a lot of anger and anxiety under the surface.

How to Help a Nine Who Is Experiencing Stress:

- Recognize their unique talents and encourage them to pursue them.
- Help them process their anger. Remind them that anger isn't always a bad thing. Use examples if possible.
- Permit them to assert themselves and their needs. Ask them to "let it all out" and remind them that this is a judgment-free zone.
- Give them some space and time to themselves.
- Remind them that it's okay to say "no" to things they don't want to do.
- Help them tune into their bodies. What do they need physically? Help them to take deep breaths.
- Go for a jog with them or engage in some other form of exercise. This will help them to de-stress and process some of their feelings.

The Enneagram and Its Symbols

The Outer Circle

The circle is the foundation of the Enneagram symbol. It represents infinity, wholeness, and the natural order of the universe. For millennia, religions have seen it as the oneness and eternal nature of God. The circle is the underlying unity in all things, even when that unity isn't visible.

The circle also represents enclosure. It creates a boundary around the personality described in its interior and opens up the possibility to move beyond the conditioned self outside of the circle. In other words, if the interior of the Enneagram symbol describes nine ways of being in the world, then the circle is there to remind us that we can choose to step outside of those into something bigger and more expansive and mysterious.

s

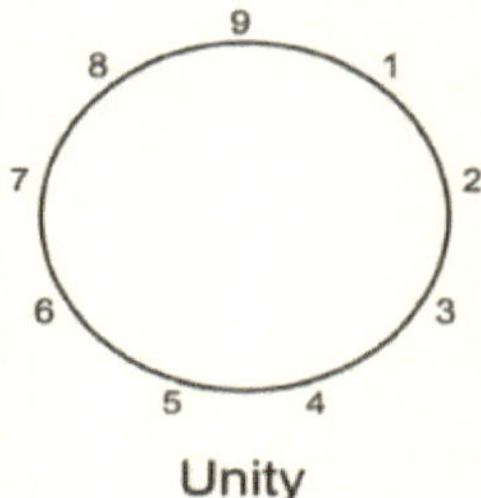

 source: Shutterstock.com

The Triangles (The Law of Three)

The inner triangle represents the three forces that must enter into all acts of creation—the active, passive, and reconciling (or neutral). Trinitarian ideas show up in most world religions, but you can think about this more simply through the idea of a sailboat. The boat is the passive force, the wind is the active force, and the sail is the reconciling force. All three forces must come into play to move our boat to where we want to go. However, we sometimes need a bit of help to recognize which force we are lacking.

The Law of Three makes up the inner triangle in the Enneagram symbol, representing the three aspects needed to bring something into being—an advancing force, a resisting force, and a reconciling force that mediates between and brings the two together.

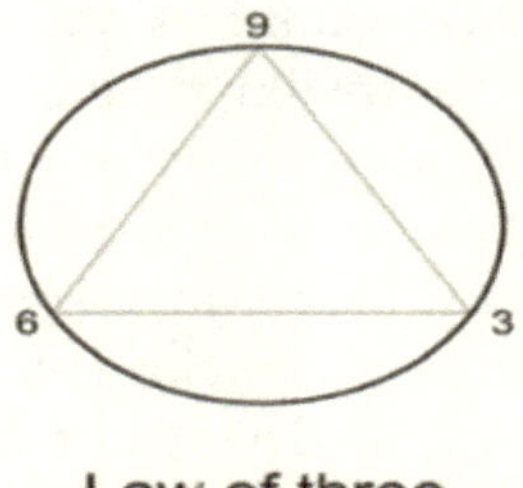

Law of three

Source: Shutterstock.com

The Hexad (The Law of Seven)

While the Law of Three describes how things come into being, the Law of Seven describes how things happen in a process or via steps. It reveals a cyclical process of transformation and reflects the idea that the only constant in the universe is change.

Movement along the arrows of the Enneagram highlights specific steps in a cycle of transformation.

Source: Shutterstock.com

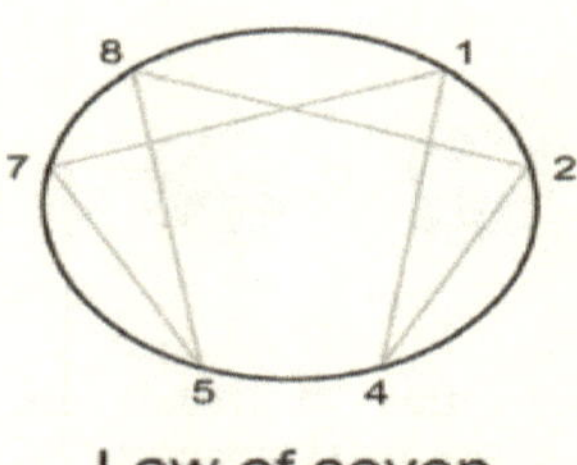

Law of seven

Personality can be seen as a form of getting stuck or fixated at one point on a natural path of change.

Therefore, according to this law, using our defense mechanisms to protect ourselves will only interfere with the natural flow or rhythm of life.

The hexad shape illustrates that nothing in life happens in a straight line, but there are always highs and lows along the way. It symbolizes the dynamic and ever-changing nature of being. Nothing is static and everything evolves or devolves, but in ways that are predictable by their nature or by the forces at play.

You can see examples of the Law of Seven in Western musical octaves, the periodic table, and the number of days in a week.

The Significance of Nine

Source: Shutterstock.com

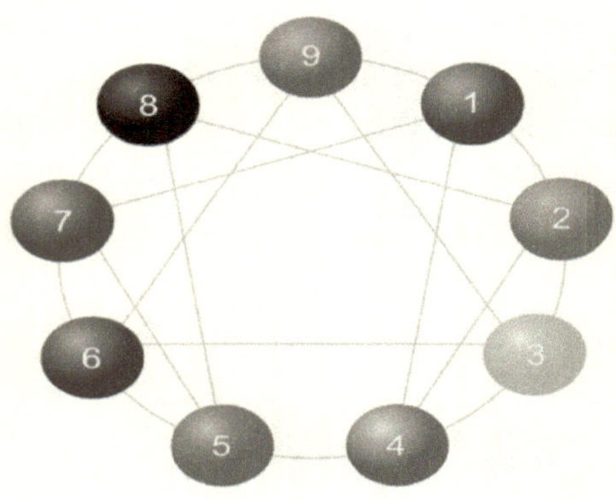

Nine is the final number in the base-10 mathematical system and it symbolizes the highest achievement in a specific endeavor. The ancient Greeks also called nine "the horizon" as it represented for them that which encloses or binds the essential elements into a whole. You can see the significance of nine in several classic texts, including the Kabbalah Tree of Life, the nine lands visited and the archetypal journey of *The Odyssey*, and in the sins or unconscious patterns that prevented people from reaching heaven in Dante's *Divine Comedy*.

When you put the symbols together, you get the Enneagram. When combined, these symbols signal a universe that is constantly changing, yet at the same time, communicates a concept of unity within the natural world. How beautiful is that?

When I first encountered the Enneagram, I felt like it articulated a deep truth that resonated with my intuitive knowing; not unlike how I felt when I read Plato's Allegory of the Cave. Once I understood its historical roots, it made sense to me. It helped me see how all this wisdom is related and likely has common roots.

It does seem as though everything changes, and the more we resist that truth, the harder life can be. It also seems as though we behave according to predictable pattern—once you know to look for them. I can see in my life that I'm prone to acting out of an unconscious state and that when I wake up to my patterns, I have the opportunity to make different choices and find perspective beyond my own cultural or family conditioning.

Each section of the Enneagram can tell us about our psychology and our spirit. The Enneagram speaks the truth about us, and helps us to understand the fundamental question of who we are and why we behave in the way that we do. Lastly, it offers suggestions to help fix any aspect of us that is broken, stressed, or overly defensive.

Wings

In short, Enneagram wings are important extensions of your core type that provide more detail about your own unique, colorful personality. In this segment, you will learn about the following:

- Each Enneagram type has two adjacent wings.
- One of the adjacent wings is more dominant than the other.
- Wings can be thought of as a continuum, rather than a fixed label.
- Your behavior and personality are influenced by wings.
- There are 18 Enneagram descriptions with core types and wings. In total, there exists 1,944 possible wing-tritype-instinctual variant combinations.

Mechanism of the Wings

Enneagram types take off (pun intended) with influences from an adjacent type. For example, a Type Two (The Helper) could take the wing of the Type One (The Reformer) or Type Three (The Achiever). Some people have influences from both possible wings—however, there's usually a stronger (i.e., dominant) wing.

Your dominant wing finds its way into your Enneagram type and acts as a sidekick to all your inner motivations and goals. Although wings are commonly referred to as "extensions" or "helpers", they hold great power to unlock the potential of your multifaceted personality. And that's where the exciting part comes in—the ability to recognize your patterns and change them!

As for notation, Enneagram wings are officially referenced to (in addition to your main Enneagram type) as "[Core Enneagram Type Number]w[Wing Number]". For example, "5w6" reads aloud as "Five Wing Six." In this case, the core Enneagram type is Five and the supporting wing is Six.

The Essence of Understanding Wings

How much do Enneagram wings matter in comparison to your core type? It's essential to understand the key ego fixations, motives, vices, and virtues of each Enneagram core type before moving on to wings (and, eventually, types as well as fixes). By understanding wings, you can gain a clearer picture of what your inner motivations look like and how they emerge from your actions and thoughts. You'll also be able to figure out which career paths align well with your interests and talents. Lastly, on top of achieving your long-term career goals, you'll be able to explore potential lifestyles and environments in which you'll thrive.

Although each of the nine Enneagram types can be influenced by both possible wings, there's often a stronger one. It's excessively rare—if not impossible—to have equally balanced wings. It's just as difficult to find a perfectly balanced ambivert who scores precisely 50/50 on the Introversion–Extraversion scale.

Distinctions between Core Type and Wings

Can your Enneagram core type exist without its wings? Wings can be thought of as on a continuum, in line with your core Enneagram type. They're attached to your core Enneagram type, which we discuss in more detail below:

Your core Enneagram type (1, 2, 3, 4, 5, 6, 7, 8, or 9) sets the framework for your behaviors and thought patterns. Your wing, on the other hand, branches out from your Enneagram roots and gives them a spinoff. It's similar to having a coffee with a vanilla or espresso shot—which makes it all the more interesting!

Examples of Wings and Behavior

Wings can significantly alter how behavior manifests in an individual. For example, a 3w2 would focus on getting ahead and acquiring a fanbase or support network (the Two wing's influence). The 3w4, in comparison, would primarily aim for originality and self-expression in their achievements (the Four wing's influence).

The same core type sporting different wings results in different preferences under the same situation. For example, a 7w6 may opt for a career in stand-up comedy to combat their inner fears and anxieties, given its Six wing. A 7w8, on the other hand, could gravitate toward travel blogging and exploring the world while maintaining a large amount of creative freedom, given its Eight wing.

You may have challenges distinguishing between two Enneagram types (with wings) in which the core Enneagram type and wing number is flipped, such as the 5w6 and the 6w5. It becomes more of a challenge if both numbers fall under the same triad (the Head triad, in this case). The 5w6 would place more value on their intellectual pursuits, whereas the 6w5 would focus on trying to eliminate their anxieties.

Fundamental Descriptions of the Wings

The wings are the Enneagram style numbers of either side of our core Enneagram style. In basic wing theory, 9 and 2 are wings for Ones, 1 and 3 are wings for Twos, 2 and 4 are wings for Threes, 3 and 5 are wings for Fours, 4 and 6 are wings for Fives, 5 and 7 are wings for Sixes, 6 and 8 are wings for Sevens, 7 and 9 are wings for Eights, and 8 and 1 are wings for Nines.

Here is the basic information on the wings for each Enneagram style and how these wings augment our core Enneagram style.

Wings for Ones

Nine Wing: Ones with a Nine wing have a greater ability to relax and unwind without having to go on vacation. They are less reactive when they disagree with someone. Plus, they are more likely to solicit the opinions of others rather than relying primarily on their own judgments or only on the judgments of those they respect.

Two Wing: Ones with a Two wing are more consistently generous and people-focused, in addition to being more gregarious and displaying more consistent warmth to others.

Wings for Twos

One Wing: When Twos have access to their One wing, they balance their focus on people with dedication to a task. They are more discerning about situations and people. They pay more attention to detail, and have an increased ability to be firm and to say no with far less worry about how others will react to them when they assert themselves in this way.

Three Wing: Twos with a Three wing are far more comfortable being visible, such as holding a high-profile leadership position. Also, these Twos feel more comfortable acknowledging their desire to be successful; in fact, they often pursue being respected as much as they do being liked.

Wings for Threes

Two Wing: Threes with Two wings are far more sensitive to the feelings of others and more generous with their time and resources. They often focus on helping others in their professional and/or personal lives.

Four Wing: Threes who have a Four wing are far more in contact with their feelings and are willing to engage in emotional conversations with others. They have a deeper personal presence and may engage in some form of artistic expression or refined level of artistic appreciation.

Wings for Fours

Three Wing: When Fours have a Three wing, they are more action-oriented, have higher and more consistent energy levels, exhibit more poise and confidence, and are more comfortable with being highly visible rather than shying away from visibility or feeling ambivalent about it.

Five Wing: Fours with a Five wing are more objective and analytical, which provides a counterpoint to their more subjective emotional way of relating with others. Also, they have an increased ability to perceive situations from a more considered and less reactive perspective. Overall, they often demonstrate more self-restraint and self-containment.

Wings for Fives

Four Wing: Fives with a Four wing are more emotionally sensitive and expressive, and also have an aesthetic perspective, perhaps engaging in the arts themselves—for example, they may write poetry, novels, or screenplays, and/or are photographers or artists.

Six Wing: Fives with a Six wing engage more readily with teams, tend to place greater value on loyalty, and may have enhanced intuitive insight. Although many other Fives can also be quite insightful, their insights come more from putting facts together and engaging in extensive analysis. When a Five has a Six wing, the insights come more quickly as the product of instantaneous processing.

Wings for Sixes

Five Wing: When Sixes have a Five wing, they are more internally than externally focused and are also more self-contained and restrained, rendering them with a tendency to be less reactive. On top of this, they have an increased passion for knowledge and use the pursuit of knowledge not only to gather information to feel prepared, but also for the pure enjoyment of learning.

Seven Wing: It is sometimes said that Sixes see the glass as half-empty and Sevens see it as half-full. So when Sixes have a Seven wing, they see the whole glass and therefore tend to be more cheerful, less worried, more optimistic, and high-energy.

Wings for Sevens

Six Wing: Sevens with a Six wing have the capacity to understand situations as being both half-full and half-empty. Because these Sevens have an increased perceptiveness and an ability to anticipate potential problems, their actions become more deliberate and less based on their instantaneous reactions.

Eight Wing: Sevens with an Eight wing tend to be more direct, assertive, and powerful. They have a more grounded presence and an increased desire to put ideas into action.

Wings for Eights

Seven Wing: Eights with a Seven wing have a lightheartedness to the usually more serious Eight outlooks, are more high-spirited and independent, and tend to be far more adventurous. They are willing to try new things in their personal and professional lives for the sake of experimentation and enjoyment.

Nine Wing: Eights with a Nine wing are interpersonally warmer, calmer, and less reactive. They solicit and listen to others' opinions because they are more consensually oriented.

Wings for Nines

Eight Wing: Nines with an Eight wing have a more take-charge orientation, exhibiting solidity and forcefulness while still maintaining a desire to hear others' opinions. With a very strong Eight wing, Nines assert their points of view more readily and make fast and clear decisions, even in the face of strong opposition.

One Wing: When Nines have a One wing, they are more attentive—for example, they pay more attention to detail, and are more punctual and precise. Although Nines often diffuse their attention, a One wing increases their overall focus, acuity, clarity, and discernment.

Other Brief Descriptions of the 18 Enneagram Types with Wings

1w9: Practical and meticulous perfectionists with a knack for catching inconsistencies in others' reasoning and judgment.

1w2: Socially aware activists and advocates who work tirelessly behind the scenes to uphold high safety standards for others.

2w1: Deeply empathetic and caring individuals who find fulfillment in others' happiness and well-being.

2w3: Outgoing and productive organizers who thrive on connecting people and being part of a group.

3w2: Socially-savvy and popular go-getters who enjoy meeting new people and networking events.

3w4: Driven and organized "bosses" always on the go with new business ideas and projects, who find great joy in efficiency and rewards.

4w3: Charismatic and individualistic artists with a sense of wonder about the underlying beauty in nature as well as of the spectrum of human emotions.

4w5: Intense and artistic creator on a mission to use self-expression to highlight the universality of the human condition.

5w4: Idiosyncratic (and often autodidactic) lone ranger who deeply values autonomy and mastery in a subject.

5w6: Detached and curious researcher who gains energy from digging into fascinating topics, under the radar.

6w5: Resourceful and dutiful team worker who highly values security and knowledge, often with a great sense of humor.

6w7: Optimistic and fun-loving explorers of life with a (somewhat contradictory) need for safety and comfort.

7w6: Happy-go-lucky and humorous experience junkie who is always on the search for new projects to undertake.

7w8: Creative and innovative entrepreneur who enjoys experimenting and creating with new mediums and ideas.

8w7: Headstrong and confident self-starter who works hard and plays hard—paired with a fearless attitude.

8w9: Servant leader who keeps others' best interests in mind to preserve harmony and gently encourages them to take action.

9w8: Independent yet calm vagabond on a (rather quiet) mission to discover what makes society a kinder and more accepting place.

9w1: Collected and pragmatic saver who values both cooperation and justice, along with the feeling of being connected to others in their community.

Modern Day Application of the Enneagram

The Enneagram and Parenting

Have you ever wondered what is the hardest thing to do? Well, it's parenting. Parenting is like a seed you plant; it needs water consistently and care, lest it wither. Concerning parenting, it is pertinent to note that you are dealing with another human being you ushered into this world—your mistakes should be their correction, your success should be their upliftment. It is a long and continuous process of nurturing your young ones till old age, when they can think and act for themselves. At this stage, a parent must be like a circle, constantly adapting to changes in their children's behavior, offering remedies to their shortcomings and stress, as well as a rewards and punishment system to keep them solidly in the family.

With the Enneagram, one has in their power a most powerful tool: empathy. The Enneagram grants you the empathy to read, analyze, and relate to people's emotions. The goal of the Enneagram is to give parents a comprehensive assessment of their children and wards in terms of their strengths and weakness, what motivates them, their biggest fears, and, at the same time, allows one to offer remedial ways in regulating kids' behavior. Aside from that, the Enneagram provides ample opportunity for one to check themselves as a parent with these questions: "Is my attitude to my kids worth sustaining, are there habits or characteristics of mine that negatively affect my kids, do my decisions cause bias or make my kids feel left out of the family…or are they inappropriate for a parent?"

The Enneagram gives accurate answers to these ranging questions with an upfront edge. With this personality tool, one can gain insight into oneself and into one's children/wards. For instance, have you ever come across this situation as described below?

Maddy's father tells her he trusts his money with her more than the rest of the family because she's meticulous, frugal in her doings, and her love for solving complicated concepts are great advantages to running the family business. He wouldn't give his money to Maddy's brother James, who, as the firstborn, is expected to take over the reins of leadership. Although James could be a helper in times of need for his siblings, he's always on the move, yearning for adventure, and his commitment to the business could come and go…not an asset for the company.

Some schools of thought have criticized the Enneagram for its one-way application, as they opined that aside from empathy, the Enneagram may introduce harsh but true doctrines that could disrupt the incumbent social and cultural settings in society. As the Enneagram is hard to master without real dedication, it may cause misappropriation of its doctrines to the ever-changing interface of human interaction. Yet, the fact remains of the Enneagram's authenticity as concerns human development. In truth, the Enneagram's doctrines do not set out to stereotype our kids or pigeonhole people. Rather, the goal is to enable them to look beneath their behaviors and those of others; understand their capabilities, their strengths, and weakness; and, ultimately, handle their responses in embracing others' point of view. If the Enneagram can be deployed during the early stages of childhood, it could help in fostering self-discovery, confidence, and better interactions with people.

The Enneagram and Education

Education, as they say, is the bedrock of a nation. As all-encompassing as this statement is, it is fair to say that a nation's growth and development is a direct result of the quality and standard of education in the institution.

Yet, the one thing everyone tends to forget is that education consists of people who teach us. And I must confess, although I'm not a career teacher, imparting knowledge to students can be very cumbersome. As a teacher, you are concerned about your student's understanding, application, and adaptation to whatever you teach. If a student passes, accolades go to you. If a student fails, the heat falls heavily on you.

In reality, teachers in typical schools (ranging from middle, college, and graduate) are facing real-life challenges. They not only have to cope with students' erratic behavior and enforce rules among students, but they are also in a constant battle with their mindset. According to Jay Hidalgo, researchers have observed that an average teacher experiences stress at twice the rate of the general population. Their burnout and stress levels are so high that they cannot help but feel overwhelmed by them. In this case, having a strong aura of awareness, empathy, and understanding is highly necessary to living and maintaining a successful career. Hence, the need for the Enneagram.

By understanding the Enneagram, you can see how things should be and how to set things right. As a personality tool, the Enneagram can offer a successful pragmatic result to various stakeholders in an educational institution. These stakeholders include the student, the teacher, school(s)/educational communities, parents, and investors.

The Enneagram and Students' Well-Being

The Enneagram offers a range of options to aid a student's well-being. First, it can equip the teacher with the knowledge of the unique personality traits that every student in the class possesses. As such, teachers can exercise due discretion and due diligence in addressing the certain tendencies in every one of their students, thereby avoiding a return to the "one size fits all" approach.

The Enneagram also offers a good communication tool and a better rapport between a student and teacher. For instance, it is common in universities for students to fear their tutors/lecturers, and for the professors to be unnecessarily rigid and strict in order to command respect from their students. The problem lies when the tutor cannot effectively communicate with all their students and ends up choosing favorites, which usually consists of those students who excel in their studies or who are similar in personality to the teacher. This ends up leaving others behind.

However, the Enneagram helps in quashing the traditional notion of "your lecturers knowing what's best for you" by introducing the concept of a healthy lecturer-student relationship in universities. Still, in the case of teacher-student relationships, the Enneagram enables a tutor to fully understand and interact with students vis-à-vis. For instance, it is common in college and in graduate schools for students to be afraid to challenge the lecturer on topics presented in the classroom. For example, types Eight and Three may be more unconventional types of students who are more assertive, future-oriented, and could be domineering due to their enthusiastic taste for knowledge. If misunderstood, they could be termed as people who want to outshine their teachers. But the truth lies in the fact that they only want to explore and, being assertive, they want to be motivated to achieve more. Conversely, type Four or Nine students can be dependent or present-oriented, though they may also be seen as lazy and so it takes a fully self-aware tutor to see otherwise. Using the Enneagram, one will understand that these personalities simply need to be given ample time and space to prepare them for their pursuit of success. Nobody is dumb or a "dunce"—it just depends on how quickly their particular personalities assimilate to the educational style used.

The Enneagram affords students a wider grasp of the world by revealing their tendencies, what motivates them to succeed, and how to gain favor from both their colleagues and tutor.

The Enneagram and Teachers' Well-Being

More often than not, a teacher who can establish healthy relationships with both their students and their colleagues is highly revered in the community. Research points out that the success or failure of students or institutions can be attributed to key players—namely, the teacher. Imparting knowledge to students isn't enough. What complements it is the drive and discipline to maintain the trend.

Speaking of discipline, the Enneagram affords teachers the opportunity to understand themselves, gain self-awareness, pinpoint their motivations and their weaknesses, and how to create an equilibrium between themselves and others. The Enneagram shines a light on both the lows and highs of their behavior. It lets them know when and how not to exhibit some behaviors, as well as raising archetypal challenges that could bring out the best in them. For instance, when stressed, Professor Milligram may yell at James, "You are not going to make it in life with this behavior!" Though the professor was stressed, how do you think this statement could affect James's mentality? James has essentially been emotionally abused, so he may decide to drop out of school because he felt what the professor said to him is true—or he may resort to illegal means to succeed academically or in life outside the classroom just to prove a point.

It is evident that there is often a disconnect that stems from being under stress. But with the full knowledge of the Enneagram, one would know how to handle unfortunate situations like this as it gives you visible and viable options to take when you are caught in a difficult, daunting, or abusive situation.

The Enneagram as a personality tool provides tutors with tools, skills, and pathways to responding to both students' and parents' needs. It also helps in making a winning team within the class. By using the Enneagram, students can be taught to work as a team, and grow awareness and even appreciation of others' different traits and needs. They can be encouraged to be adaptive of each others' tendencies, thereby building healthy team cohesion.

The Enneagram and Leadership

"Everyone is a born leader."

This is what the Enneagram will teach you first. Greatness is not reserved for those with so-called birthrights or royal affiliation. In fact, leadership is a mindset, and with the right one, you can achieve anything. Through the Enneagram, we are introduced to our personality type and what it reveals about us. On the road to greatness, the Enneagram creates an aura of responsibility in us that helps us face life's hurdles with courage and relate better with our peers in a way that could assert our reliability and competence, without revealing overbearing or domineering tendencies that could be detrimental to our relationships.

Although we all have the nine types within us, one is dominant, and with that dominant type comes its own set of unique gifts and challenges. By understanding your type, you can let go of habitual patterns and open up to your inherent gifts. As you become more aware of your type, you can complete levels of growth and ultimately lead with your best self. You can understand your reactions to things, your preferences, and how to be part of a well-adjusted team.

With this level of self-awareness, we can be free of the patterns that hold us back and develop an understanding of those with whom we interact.

Type One: The Reformer

Type One leaders get the job done, allowing little to no room for error. Trusting that others can carry out tasks to meet their standards is challenging for Ones, which results in their difficulty delegating tasks. If you're a One, as you become more aware of this pattern, mentor others. Trust their abilities and value their input, relieving yourself of the burden of doing it all yourself.

Type 2: The Helper

Type Two leaders can get caught in their need to be seen as helpful. Their people-pleasing behaviors, such as flattery and being overly generous, can often get in the way of their taking a firm stand when it's needed. If you're a Two and want to be an effective and truly selfless leader, let go of the need to take care of everyone else and make your own needs an equal priority.

Type 3: The Achiever

When type Three leaders aren't aware of their personality type, they live and lead in reaction to an unconscious belief that they are worthless. That is, they are always trying to prove themselves. They strive for validation by overachieving, often becoming outstanding in their fields, yet it's frequently at the expense of their relationships and emotions.

If you're a Three, get in touch with yourself and accept that your value comes from who you are—not what you do. You can be an authentic and inspiring leader without needing to be the "shining star." Relax into a more motivational role so you can benefit the team and the organization.

Type 4: The Individualist

Type Four leaders often struggle with fitting in with their families, organizations, or in society at large, believing that they are somehow flawed. To compensate for this belief, they set themselves apart by identifying themselves as "special" or "unique."

If you're a Four and want to be an effective leader, you must let go of your story and step into a sense of belonging to your team and organization. As you do so, bring your gift of creativity forth, making you an intuitive and gifted leader.

Type Five: The Investigator

Type Five leaders often appear detached from the team; however, they're observing every detail. They have an unconscious fear of being inadequate or unable to function in the world. They are extremely intelligent. They become experts in one area and connect to the group using this expertise, resulting in confidence. If you're a Five, use your clarity as a strength and let it benefit those around you.

Type Six: The Loyalist

Loyalists are the glue that holds the team together. They're excellent troubleshooters and have a plan for every possible worst-case scenario. This strategizing comes from their lack of trust that they are supported in return. At their best, Loyalists let go of their skepticism and lead from a place of trust. It allows them to shine in their ability to pay attention to the details that need to be addressed for the team to be successful. Sixes are natural leaders; however, they don't want all the credit.

Type Seven: The Enthusiast

Type Seven leaders are visionaries, endlessly generating new ideas. They have an insatiable appetite for new experiences and a fear of missing out on them. Thus, they pursue many activities and experiences with abandon. Their challenge is carrying their brilliant ideas to fruition, as they're easily distracted by the next great project. If you're a Seven, your awareness of this fact will help you prioritize and focus your efforts. You'll step into your true gift of delivering a brilliant vision for your team and organization.

Type Eight: The Challenger

Type Eight leaders can engage in bullying when they feel their sense of control is threatened. They may become willful, vengeful, or demanding. But when they can relax, knowing their control is not being threatened, they're able to connect through their heart and vulnerability. At their best, Eights are strong leaders with magnanimous hearts.

Type Nine: The Peacemaker

Type Nine leaders, generally easygoing and kind, have an unconscious need for peace and harmony, which can result in them overlooking problems that impact the organization. Nines tend to withdraw and disengage when faced with conflict. When Nines are unaware of these tendencies within themselves, their teams become frustrated with their inability to step in and take a stand.

Nines shine as leaders when they can maintain their serene nature while also engaging in and dealing with the reality of what the team is facing. At their best, they lead with a peaceful and grounded style.

The Enneagram and Psychology

The Enneagram's impact on all human endeavors is far-reaching. The application of this personality tool to psychology has yielded many results and insights into the study of human behavior. Indeed, psychiatrists and psychologists have utilized many systems for describing personality characteristics and styles. These empirical methods may have varied widely in their basis, acceptance, and application, but this has not deterred the efficacy of the Enneagram. In fact, in the past, the Enneagram was reputed to have been used alongside some personality test tools such as the Myers Briggs, the Sutton analysis, etc.

In recent times, extensive research on the Enneagram has paved the way for conducting an accurate analysis of a patient's behavior through the advanced use of a personality test like the Riso-Hudson Enneagram Type Indicator (RHETI), a tool used in the Diagnostic and Statistical Manual of Mental Disorder (DSM-5), which is likewise used for evaluating behaviors. Some have proposed that the Enneagram is a more comprehensive model for personality than what is currently adopted in the DSM-5.

As an addendum in discussing the DSM-5, its alternative model of personality disorders is identical to the Enneagram. It identifies disruptions by unique characteristics and states that each is stable and healthy. Each form of personality will correspond to one of the ten DSM-5 personality disorders (if unhealthy) in these proposed models. For example, an unstable individual with a personality of type Three may demonstrate narcissistic personality disorder. Many scholars, including Naranjo, have indicated that this idea was validated but little research has been done. Moreover, certain forms of personalities lead to such disorders. For example, anyone who fits the requirements for a narcissistic personality disorder cannot classify themselves as someone of a type Three character. This is an important field for further research as it would allow personality disorders to be treated more broadly with new ideas.

Although several leaders use the Enneagram for personal development, some clinicians have used it in more conventional psychotherapies. Therapists use it, for example, to help patients or clients understand their central motivations and influential defense mechanisms, or to speak about objects. Again, research on this particular usefulness is minimal, but current studies indicate that the Enneagram can be a handy tool. It seems likely to help formulate an argument, at least.

The different aspects and the complex relationships between the types of personalities seem normal for questions about the worldview, the security of Egos, the relationships between things, core beliefs, interpersonal dynamics, and the consciousness of the patient. Even though not placed squarely in this space, a therapist may help by asking questions or taking into account the nuanced patterns that fit within the Enneagram system.

The Enneagram and Crime

In this world of ours, there are three-dimensional phases of humans. The first phase is our trying to discover oneself, the second is knowing what benefits us (our means to eternal happiness), and the third is the means to consolidate it.

We have long tried to find the means to achieving eternal joy and happiness in life. However, the means of achieving such are far-fetched. For this reason, we have to put in everything we have to achieve this, and more importantly, we can clash with conflicting interests from our peers that may hinder our own.

For instance, Joe feels he could live the American dream of happiness if he has a lot of money. Thus, he saves more, works harder, and takes on more work for extra profit (even if he knows this extra work will affect his business relationships with his clients). This same determination could manifest differently in Chris, who may decide instead to sell illegal drugs or rob innocent people of their valuables to satisfy his flashy lifestyle.

Observing these two examples solidifies the true motives for the crime, and in their own best interests, they resort to indulging in these activities. Unfortunately, it is important to note that the first category of people who are yet to discover themselves constitutes the major chunk of people who are in the business of perpetuating crime or are the recipients of it. Take, for instance, Cindy, who comes from a broken home. She feels depressed and unsure of who she is, and her environment is also nothing to write home about. As a result, she resorts to taking hard drugs to ease the pain of her existence and so begins her battle with drug addiction. Cindy's story begs the question: what can the Enneagram do in preventing these unfortunate events?

The Enneagram personality model, as an applied approach, provides an accurate map of the mental structure of an individual. According to this system, different personality patterns are metaphors for the individual's active psychological functions. The Enneagram is considered a suitable model for improving self-scrutiny when facing stressful situations. This system can contribute to the formation of safe intellectual and behavioral patterns, and prevent the individual from committing risky behaviors.

The Enneagram could work out in two ways to suppress crime. The first way is acting as a precautionary measure in addressing issues of lost identities, managing temperamental tendencies, and showing a path to a purposeful life. The second way, on the other hand, aids people who are deep into crime, such as inmates or ex-convicts who are at a crossroads. It helps these people know that the life they live is a result of their stress, and if they continue to live under the direction of their stress, the way to peace will be a long journey that they'll never realize.

In the study of the Enneagram and its application to crime, it can be seen as a cursory analysis of the rationales for which people commit crimes. At this stage, I have to make it clear that while an Enneagram cannot instruct one how to live their life (a faulty notion, as stereotypical as it is), it can be used as an informative tool in guiding one to self-awareness. Secondly, the Enneagram simplifies the vulnerability of humans to crime, irrespective of how appealing your number type (or your wing) finds subversive action.

For instance, a type Two may decide to shield an armed robber from the police because she feels empathy toward him, even if she knows she's commiting the crime of obstructing justice. Or a Five may refuse to report sensitive information about an enemy country to his government because he thinks he could profit from it.

One thing that the Enneagram has unified are the differences in petty crime and harder crime. In its tenets, it doesn't matter what one indulges in, but it is not the pathway to greatness nor self-discovery.

Although beautiful in its principles, the Enneagram has lately been overshadowed by religious doctrines and spiritualism that tend to blend their beliefs with the practical use of it. So in order to preserve the Enneagram as an essential tool, recipients need an in-depth understanding of what it entails. By doing so, it will be easy to spot an adulterated doctrine.

There may also be a misunderstanding about the fundamental characteristics of how the types function. Let's take, for example, types One and Eight. These types are both in the instinctive triad, and are both strong and actorial—plus, both have strong notions of how to do things. Overall, they are both strong and determined. However, Ones will try, from the point of view of a moral imperative, to persuade others to do the right thing (at least as they see it). They try but become annoyed and less rational when others oppose their thinking. They do not understand the other. On the other hand, Eights depend on their self-confidence and try using their shrewd ideas and pure personal charm to influence others. Altogether, Ones strive to persuade those who oppose them while Eights try to power through them—"I don't know if it's the right way, but it's *my* way."

The main confusion between these two types involves their concern for justice, although their sense of justice can be somewhat different. To Ones, justice is an incredibly valuable principle for many judges and lawyers. Ones also think a lot about the problems of adequate human standards and how a fair and equal framework can be enforced. Justice is at all stages of growth and Ones feel that they are always after pure justice (no matter how skewed their interpretation of it may become). In this way, Ones are looking for justice and would like to fix injustices wherever they encounter them.

For Eights, justice is more of a primal reaction—that is, a reaction to injustice. Eights, in general, don't care about these problems. But if they saw a vulnerable person being hurt and injured by others, Eights would rush to level the playing field without hesitation. Eights look upon themselves as protectors of others and they keep their team safe. Eights strive to pursue justice for "their people"—their families, friends, employers, ethnic groups, and so on. Eights are also articulate in the interests of equality of those for whom they believe they are responsible. This more limited interest in injustice can be seen in the story of Robin Hood. Robin Hood isn't trying to overthrow the king or the sheriff, but he is trying to even out the balance of power and money by helping the poorest of his community. In fact, with Eights, their sense of justice generally requires coping with a power imbalance.

Naturally, all negative actions in regard to justice may be grossly unfair in their unhealthy manifestations. Some people may always believe they are rational—the sanctions they enforce are for the benefit or, at least, for the good of society. They believe their punitive actions need to be rationalized. Eights, as it turns out, do not. The administration of justice for unsafe Eights only offers revenge ("Andy has ripped me off. Now he must pay."). Some will doubt the "justice" of either of these forms of behavior—"You hurt me or my people, and I'm going to destroy you.").

Career Opportunities for Enneagram Personalities

This segment talks about the select jobs that are suitable for each personality. It is also pertinent to note that while these job opportunities are suggested, it is not imposing on you to start looking for these kinds of jobs as soon as you're done with college on the basis that you have fully discovered yourself through the Enneagram. Yet, the Enneagram will teach you to be critical, analytical, and more embracing of yourself in making your career decisions.

What are the best careers for Type One personalities?

There are tons of jobs in which the Reformer type would excel. But here are seven jobs to get you started.

Professors: Type One personalities are "well-organized, orderly, and fastidious", according to the Enneagram Institute. They aim to maintain high standards and, as professors, uphold those standards in schools. Because they're also purposeful, being specialists in their fields allows them to help teach undergraduate and graduate students to be professors, with intentions to help their students grow into careers similar to their own.

Judges: Type One personalities believe in the truth, maintain objectivity, and have a lot of integrity. For that reason, they make great judges. "Extremely principled, always want to be fair, objective, and ethical: truth and justice primary values. Sense of responsibility, personal integrity and of having a higher purpose often make them teachers and witnesses to the truth," according to the Enneagram Institute.

Police officers: Again, because Ones care so much about upholding standards, they make dedicated police officers who uphold the law.

Environmental specialists: Type One personalities are the reformist types who want to create change and do well in jobs that serve a purpose—especially a purpose about which they're passionate. As environmental specialists, they can help make an impact on the entire world.

Activist: One personalities are passionate and purposeful. They have an intense sense of right and wrong as part of their personal beliefs, and they're willing to fight for what's right and what they wholeheartedly believe in.

Social workers: Type One personality types make phenomenal social workers because they crave making an impact on others' lives. They tend to be realistic and know the best next steps, and they can help others take those steps and turn their lives around.

Detectives: Type One personalities are obsessed with the truth. And, as detectives, they can spend their entire career digging for it.

What are the best careers for type Two personalities?

It comes as little surprise that Twos naturally excel at working with others, especially in service-oriented capacities. They are here to make an impact and to share their effusive love with others. Below are some career paths that this personality type would find particularly fitting:

Teacher: Many Twos will feel drawn toward careers in education, where they can forge meaningful, face-to-face connections with the people they're helping and guiding every day. The formative type of impact you're able to make on people's lives in this field, whether your students are children or adults, is perhaps unparalleled.

Psychotherapist: Empathetic above all, Twos make ideal candidates for a career in psychotherapy, where their sincere, compassionate natures, and willingness to dive into the emotional archeology of others will be well-placed. The help you're able to offer as a professional in this field can truly be transformative and even life-saving.

Midwife: This type of job provides physical, emotional, and informational support to women before, during, and after childbirth, but there are other kinds of midwives as well, including ones who provide support during miscarriages and grieving processes. The endlessly caring nature of Twos makes them an ideal fit for any of these paths.

Non-profit founder: Twos are known for having a few (or 20) social causes that they feel deeply about, as well as an urge to solve the world's problems. By founding an organization dedicated to addressing such an issue, Twos can find fulfillment in feeling as connected to a cause that helps others as they possibly can, day in and day out.

Social worker: A career in social work makes perfect sense for the heart-on-their-sleeve Two, allowing them to help people in ways others cannot. Whether you're working within the spheres of substance abuse, child and family needs, or trauma, careers within this field aren't the easiest, but they can be incredibly rewarding. Ultimately, you'll know you're serving as a source of strength to some of the people who need it most.

Politician: Twos aren't necessarily the Enneagram type that will feel most innately drawn to a career in politics, but they're perhaps the type of politician the world needs most. Motivated by a genuine desire to help others and achieve the greatest good, politics is an area where Twos can achieve true, comprehensive change while helping those in need. There may be sacrifices involved and some Twos will miss the ability to do more hands-on work with the people they're helping. But the impact they can make in this field can't be argued with.

Life coach: The "We can do this—I'll help you!" attitude of Twos, as well as their propensity for giving advice, means that they would likely excel working within a coaching capacity. With an ability to step into others' shoes and intuit their truest needs and drives, empathy makes for a wonderful tool within this career field—and Twos have empathy in spades. They'll also enjoy feeling depended upon by clients, as well as finding joy in celebrating their clients' successes.

What are the best careers for type Three personalities?

Attorney: Threes make great attorneys because of the intellectual challenge posed by the field. A job in the legal field also allows them to have a global influence using a macro way of thinking and a measurable approach. This allows them to track their successes as they experience them, and requires validation and agreement as a measure of achievement.

Agent: Threes fare well as agents, whether it be literary, real estate, sports, etc. The responsibility of acting on behalf of another party allows them to channel their "performer" energy and poses the appropriate challenge for Threes who want to play an active role in achieving a certain goal.

Executive: Being an executive means having the power to enact laws, make calls to action, or create plans of attack. For an Enneagram type who likes to take charge, this career gives them the power—and exigency—to aggressively reach and exceed their goals.

Coach: Coaches may not play the game, but they have the highest say in how the game is played. This is right up a Three's alley because it lets them take control and delegate action, and allows them to witness the progression or digression of a team's success.

News journalist: It's a journalist's job to get the inside scoop on what's hot, what's new, and what's happening so they can get everyone in the know. Therefore, a career in journalism gives Threes the authority and popularity they need to feel accomplished and validated.

Actor: A career in the arts requires performance and achievement, which is Three energy at its core. Acting is one route, but the Achiever could also thrive in other performance-based roles such as singing, dancing, and stand-up comedy. Plus, a standing ovation is just the validation they need to continue pushing further.

Producer: A producer's responsibility is to oversee the production of music or film, so Threes strike a balance between control and performance in this role. Threes will appreciate the opportunity to engage in the construction, direction, and delivery of a work of art, and get their validation from the audience engagement that comes after seeing the movie.

What are the best careers for type Four personalities?

There are tons of jobs in which the creative Four would excel. But here are seven careers to get you started:

Musicians: Four personalities are so creative that it's only natural they make great musicians. They have an ear for it and are skilled at creating it.

Poets: Because Four personalities are so introspective, their creativity flows from within. As such, they make talented poets.

Journalists: Four personalities make excellent journalists, as they have creative writing skills and can also empathize well with (and, therefore, establish rapport with) sources. They do best when they're reporting on topics about which they're passionate.

Activists: Again, because Four personalities are so empathetic, they care deeply about others and causes. They use a lot of different creative outlets, music/journalism/street art/etc., to fight for what they believe in.

Painters: Four personalities are downright creative and, therefore, make skilled painters. They're also easily inspired people, which helps fuel their painting careers.

Graphic designers: Graphic designers need to be able to understand people (their clients) and then work with them to create unique designs that tell stories. There's no better personality type to do just that than a Four.

Chefs: Cooking is a creative outlet for a lot of people. It also is therapeutic for introspective people who value their alone time. As such, Four personalities make talented chefs.

What are the best careers for type Five personalities?

Medical scientists: Medical scientists must have a doctoral degree or a medical degree. The focus of their work is research and their objective is to produce medical data or materials that can be used to treat specific illnesses or improve peoples' health. They spend a lot of their time performing studies related to their research and testing the effectiveness of medications and devices. Since Enneagram Five personalities prefer working in small groups and enjoy research, they will find that this type of career provides ideal working conditions and tasks that favor this personality type's analytical strengths.

Technical writers: Technical writers normally need a bachelor's degree in communications or a comparable subject area. They produce technical written materials that explain how a product works, how to use a specific product, or how a product should be assembled. They spend a lot of time researching the products so that they understand what they're writing about, and then combine written data and technical illustrations to produce informative manuals. This is a good career option for Five personalities because technical writers spend a lot of time working independently while they research and write about the product.

Judges and hearing officers: Judges and hearing officers review evidence and information about legal matters, maintain order during legal proceedings, and may also be involved in providing a ruling or resolving a dispute between parties. They normally need to have a law degree and usually have prior legal experience gained by working as a lawyer. Judges and hearing officers can spend a lot of time reading and reviewing legal materials, listening to testimony, and assessing the information that's presented. These duties are ideal for individuals with an Enneagram Five personality because they like to study things in detail and think things through before reaching informed conclusions.

Industrial engineers: Industrial engineers assess how products are made and help identify ways to change the production process so that it is more efficient. They must monitor the production process and analyze a lot of data to develop informed conclusions. This is another career that may suit Enneagram Five personalities because it doesn't involve constant social interaction and emphasizes the need for strong research and analytical skills, since industrial engineers spend a lot of time gathering and processing data. A bachelor's degree in industrial engineering or a similar discipline is required.

Market research analysts: Market research analysts are required to have a bachelor's or master's degree in a discipline such as market research. This is a career that emphasizes strong analytical skills, which is ideal for Five personalities since they typically have excellent analytical skills. Market research analysts study factors related to market conditions for merchandise. They use statistical analysis in their work and spend a lot of time analyzing data before producing reports about their recommendations for products that should be developed and identifying the target audience for those products.

Political scientists: Political scientists assess public opinion about specific policies and how they're viewed by the public. They also research policies and determine how they will impact society. They typically study political science or a comparable discipline and must have a master's or doctoral degree in this field. This is a good career option for Fives who are more interested in the humanities because this occupation emphasizes researching and analyzing data, and developing conclusions from that research.

What are the best careers for type Six personalities?

There are tons of jobs in which the Loyalist type would excel. But here are seven careers to get you started:

Teachers: Type Six personalities value knowledge, are creative, and are devoted to helping others. For that reason, they make ideal teachers. After all, they're known as a loyal type who is dedicated to supporting others. They also value security, so they tend to be invested in the secure futures of their students.

Caretakers: Because Six personalities are so loyal, they make excellent and reliable caretakers. Their basic desire is to feel security and support, and because they understand this longing, they're able to provide it for others, too. Plus, because they sometimes have problems with self-doubt, devoting their time to investing in others' well-being may help their own well-being.

Environmental specialists: Type Six personalities care a lot about their passions. As such, becoming an environmental specialist makes sense for them. They can pour their energy into saving the planet and doing work that benefits the greater good—something that they believe in. Beyond that, because Sixes are so adept at foreseeing problems, they can develop plans for the planet that are preventative rather than solely reactive.

Security guards: Again, because Six personalities are loyal types, they make reliable security guards. They're known for their courage and how well they look out for others, after all.

Au pair: Six personalities are the best type for looking after others since they're so dependent and trustworthy. These are, perhaps, two of the most necessary qualities in an au pair.

Veterinarians: Veterinarians care deeply about animals and Six personalities make great vets. Plus, as Sixes can sometimes struggle with self-doubt, working with animals has been proven to ease stress.

Executive assistant: An executive assistant needs to be reliable and well-trusted for the top people at a company, who need to feel comfortable sharing their personal and professional lives with this person and to depend on them. And that's exactly what type Six is known for being. Beyond that, a job as an executive assistant is usually a secure one, which is comforting for Sixes.

What are the best careers for type Seven personalities?

Fitness instructor: To be a fitness instructor is to work with lots of people and to bounce away from personal odds, making it an ideal profession for any type Seven. Fitness instructors appear to have flexible timetables that change regularly, which is perfect for the ambitious Seven who is searching for a balanced work-life balance to follow other experiences. Fitness instructors are simultaneously praised for motivation and strength, thereby making them a great success for the Enthusiast of the Enneagram.

Event planner: An event planner's work is swift and project-oriented, and it tends to evolve depending on the customers, year, and other factors. The agile and entertaining Seven, who loves this type of challenge, is in great condition for it (until they get bored with it). Often, event planners directly face the customer, making good use of the charisma and excitement of the Seven. Plus, this job often involves glamorous event preparation—something that type Sevens would happily praise in conversation.

Flight attendant: Flight attendants often travel to fresh and exciting locations, which makes it an ideal career for the adventurous personality of type Seven. Between the excitement of flying to London or Amsterdam, and watching people, becoming a flight attendant will fuel the enthusiasm of Sevens to make even the routines of the job satisfying for them. Furthermore, the shift patterns and free flights give Sevens the means to alleviate their wanderlust,

Businessman: You're probably thinking of a Seven when you think of an entrepreneur. The individualism of a Seven allows them to dream of an outstanding business strategy. Their magnetism, keen intellect, and resilience likewise offer them the instruments they need for their business to succeed. Sevens will love the excitement of becoming a contractor. Furthermore, every type Seven needs the versatility to be consumed with their work when they feel the urge and take a break when they are bored.

Blogger: Like being an entrepreneur, working as a blogger is a difficult field to succeed in and for which to prepare a schedule. In addition to the excitement and versatility of blogging, a type Seven loves to do genuine and customized work. The vision of a Seven's paradise is being able to share their stories with others. And if it means dressing up and getting free stuff, then so much the better!

Life coach: Sevens are natural visionaries and are ideal candidates for life coaches. They have an uncommon ability to look at the larger picture with their idealism. As such, they will be easily able to educate others on how to fully live their lives, and they focus on the good among people. Combine a Seven's creative spirit with those skills and they have everything that is needed for a good life coach.

Publicist: Advertisers are always busy completing task after task, running to press events, or releasing hot new items. While some personalities can burn out with this hectic lifestyle, a Seven thrives in such fast-paced environments. Therefore, a publicist is an ideal profession for a Seven, ranging from thrilling ventures, a constantly evolving schedule, to having the capacity to display their charm to a customer.

What are the best careers for type Eight personalities?

The Challenger type will succeed in many different jobs. However, there are seven listed here to get you moving.

Activists: Since the characteristics of an Eight make them so secure in themselves and their thoughts, they naturally attract support from others. They are vocal leaders who make great insurgents. With their commanding attitude and assertiveness, they can often command a huge number of faithful followers to influence a government's policy and decision.

Military personnel: Many service veterans are remembered as heroes. And several Eight personalities have these qualities: "Courageous and willing to put self in serious jeopardy to achieve their vision and have a lasting influence", which is what the military is looking for. Many Eights may achieve true heroism and historical greatness through their actions on the battlefield.

Program managers: Type Eight people are influential leading figures, and program managers must be so in order to administer whole projects and supervise multiple teams. Eights are typically able to lead—an important attribute for this mission.

Executives: Again, Eights make natural leaders because they are so good at taking charge. In brief, two qualities the executive role requires are decisiveness and authority.

Athletes: Eight personalities tend to be highly competitive. As such, they make talented athletes who get motivated and stand out from others in big games.

Sales Representatives: More often than not, Eight people are competitive, they fit well in highly competitive sales situations. They also don't become overly emotional when sales don't always go down, as many sales reps do when they struggle to sell.

Governors: As natural-born leaders, type Eight personalities can make dogged governors who are able to make authoritative decisions with a can-do attitude and passion.

What are the best careers for type Nine personalities?

Tons of jobs occur in which the form of a mediator is desperately needed. Here are seven below to get you moving.

Yoga & meditation instructors: Since type Nine personalities can generally achieve mind-body connection, they can help others by teaching yoga and meditation to achieve the same state.

Alternative healers: Nines have a deep connection to themselves and an inherent capacity to listen, handle, and develop inner stability. As such, they are the sort to help others holistically rather than just medically.

Social Workers: Again, since the Nine personality is linked with healing others, they can communicate and support those who are suffering emotionally. As such, the job of a social worker is a great way for them to get out and help.

Human resource managers: Nines are brilliant at preserving peace and order. They could serve as human resources administrators, who have to do this with the fewest possible disruptions to the business.

Religious workers: Type Nine figures appear to be spiritual people, interested in religion and willing to help other individuals discover their religious curiosities. They could be bishops, pastors, or Muslim clerics as they have a persuasive and mild personality.

Caretakers: Nine personalities care a lot about other people so it's easy to see them managing houses and estates, and coming in to check on the well-being of the properties and people. They are natural guardians and make others feel safe.

Counselors: Again, Nines care so much about others and are so capable of creating internal harmony that they give excellent guidance to their clients on achieving the same kind of peace.

Enneagram Type CompatibilityTtheory

Because of the Enneagram system's hyper-attunement to our limitations, triggers, and pitfalls, knowing your Enneagram type can help you understand how to compassionately self-manage and relate to other types. Doing this Enneagram work pulls back the curtain on the inner workings of your romantic partnerships and recommends a path for growth.

After people learn their Enneagram type, the next questions I invariably get asked are: "Which types go well together?" or "Which type should I be with?" Everyone wants to know.

The answer is that all types of combinations can be happy together if both partners have high levels of self-awareness—though the reverse can also be true. All type combinations may struggle if both people have a lack of self-awareness. Therefore, type compatibility is more about similar levels of self-awareness than it is about personality type. The basic guidelines are:

- Two highly independent individuals are most likely to succeed.
- Two highly un-self-aware people may continue in a relationship, but the relationship is often marked by problems. They do not have a real chance of success.

In certain situations, the relationship typically stops making sense if one person is very self-confident and the other is not. Both people would not fully understand each other to proceed. That being said, certain relationships tend to occur more often.

The Most Common Enneagram Matches for Couples

In finding answers to this theory, we draw analysis from Hall's *The Enneagram in Love* and Helen Palmer's *The Enneagram in Love & Work* to find famous Enneagram pairings below. Hall notes that her research has shown that there are some relationship combinations that are more common, but that they are not inherently compatible.

Ones Commonly Pair Well with Twos and Sevens

Type Ones are called the Reformers of the Enneagram. Dedicated and perfectionist, these people with their high expectations are thorough and conscientious. Those who can help them lighten up and see the beauty in the imperfect times of life are attractive to them.

As Ones are task-oriented people who can feel static in a one-on-one relationship, Twos can help them to relax. Similarly, Twos, who struggle with abandonment issues, bring stability and security.

There is also something called a reciprocal relationship in a One-Seven partnership, as it shares an Enneagram axis. Ones are drawn to a Seven's irreverent, adventurous nature. The usually steady, hardworking One should remind the cheerful Seven to let go and, above all, to not be guilty of having fun. Overall, Ones infuse Sevens with an urgent sense of mission and direction, which underpins the Seven flight.

Twos Commonly Pair Well with Threes and Eights

Type Twos are classified as the Helpers of the Enneagram. Their compassion and self-sacrificing nature will give and give to their partner until they are empty. Since Twos often have difficulty vocalizing their desires, they must date someone who will not take advantage of their kindness and can reciprocate their intimacy.

In a Two-Three relationship, there are shared interests, energy levels, and charisma, making for a high-energy match. The charming Threes will galvanize the Twos to fulfill their potential rather than overrelying on others, while Twos give their Three partners unconditional acceptance and help them discover their authentic self hidden behind their public face.

There are several parallels in a Two-Eight relationship since these types share an Enneagram thread. Twos like the strength and conviction of the Eights, who remind Twos to take over and stand strong.

Threes Commonly Pair Well with Nines

Threes are known as the Achievers of the Enneagram. They are motivated, optimistic, and compelling, and are interested in excellence, breaking down their targets and achieving their ideal results. Their public-driven identity, however, can cause weakness and a lack of credibility.

In a relationship, Nines can help the goals of the Threes and, above all, profoundly embrace them for who they are rather than what they can do. With the Nine's consistency, Threes will interact with their emotions. Threes also embrace the happy-go-lucky Nine, push them to focus, and show appreciation for them. Altogether, Threes usually go hand in hand with Nines.

Fours Commonly Pair Well with Fives and Nines

Type Fours are regarded as the Enneagram's Individualists. Authenticity and strength are the traits of sensible Fours, who are also self-aware, artistically inclined, and introspective. Fours prefer to be swept away in their daydreams and emotions, which can inspire them and make them pursue more enhanced emotional conditions.

In a Four-Five relationship, Fours will maintain their emotional expression with the easy, steady Five. The rational nature of Fives can be a foundation for Fours, who can sometimes feel turbulent. Fours appreciate that Fives are not afraid of experiencing the depths and togetherness of emotions. Fours and Fives can have an intense and stimulating bond.

Fours add enthusiasm and intensity to the "Mother" Nines in a Four-Nine relationship. Nines are naturally open and welcome all emotions.

Fives Commonly Pair Well with Ones and Twos

The Investigators of the Enneagram are called Type Fives. Five are intelligent, inquiring, objective, and analytical. They enjoy learning and gaining new knowledge. Owing to their mental concentration and their ability to reside in the mind, it can be longer for a Five to process feelings and convey affection, which can come as a separation.

Fives find meaning in the freedom, curiosity, and the shared interests of the Ones in a Five-One relationship. Also, Ones love the lack of judgment and constancy of Fives, and it comforts them. The Five-One relationship will provide a solid base for trust and reliability.

There is a real meeting of opposites in a Five-Two relationship. The objectivity of Fives and their clear boundaries attract vulnerable Twos, who often find it difficult to define their limits. The autonomous Fives look for time alone and do not always want to expand and help the Twos, which forces Twos to take care of themselves.

Sixes Commonly Pair Well with Nines

Sixes are known as the Loyalists of the Enneagram. The security-oriented Sixes, dedicated and trustworthy, may be extremely nervous and skeptical, putting value in the protection of systems and organizations. They maintain calm and stable relationships.

There is a complementary and good relationship in a Six-Nine partnership. The hospitality of Nines is usually calm and friendly, which calms the eternal suspicions of Sixes. In exchange, Sixes carry the combination of unambiguous loyalty and predictability while enabling Nines to come forward and step into life.

Sevens Commonly Pair Well with Nines

Sevens are known as the Enthusiasts of the Enneagram. The playful and adventurous Sevens want life to be a jam-packed adventure. Sevens, however, are forward-looking, and in the present moment, they find they are afraid of the anxiety they are escaping, which can make them impulsive.

The free-spirited Sevens and cozy Nines are a sunny and optimistic partnership in a Seven-Nine relationship. Energetic Sevens can make the partnership dynamic, while Nines can allow Sevens to slow down and enjoy the current moment

Eights Commonly Pair Well with Nines

Eights are known as the Challengers of the Enneagram. The authoritative Eights, strong and confident, dominate their truth and communicate their love by protecting and strengthening. They can come off as vigorous and too violent because they don't reverse conflict.

Eights exude brilliant energy and skill in an Eight-Nine relationship, which attracts Nines, who appear to fuse with powerful personalities. Nines admire the willingness of the Eights to confront obstacles while the Eights take comfort in the peaceful energy of the Nines.

Nines Commonly Pair Well with Ones and Twos

Nines are known as the Peacemakers of the Enneagram. Confident and harmonious, Nines embrace loss, and can eliminate and simplify issues through their conflict-averse existence. Nines may become too relaxed, which can lead to a stubborn reluctance to stake any claim.

In their relationship, the simple existence of Ones profits Nines immensely. Reciprocally, when Ones are suffering from extreme criticism, the gentle, friendly Nines will reduce their fears that they should always be right. On the other hand, Ones should provide peaceful Nines with structure and clarification.

Both types may feel identical in how they communicate and how they respond in a Nine-Two relationship. The good-natured Nines love Twos, and not just for what all the support Twos can offer. Rather, Nines are free to invest emotionally in Twos, encouraging them to set goals and to take an active part in their lives.

Also, see Lynn Ruolo's research: http://www.9types.com/writeup/enneagram_relationships.php

Most Common Match If:	
A woman is Type 1 (Reformer)	Man is Type 9 (Peacemaker)
A woman is Type 2 (Helper)	Man is Type 8 (Leader)
The woman is Type 3 (Achiever)	Man is Type 1 (Perfectionist)
A woman is Type 4 (Artist)	Man is Type 9 (Peacemaker)

A woman is Type 5 (Thinker)	Man is Type 1 (Perfectionist)
A woman is Type 6 (Loyalist)	Man is Type 8 (Leader) or Type 9 (Peacemaker)
A woman is Type 7 (Enthusiast)	Man is Type 5 (Thinker) or Type 1 (Perfectionist)
A woman is Type 8 (Leader)	Man is Type 9 (Peacemaker)
A woman is Type 9 (Peacemaker)	Man is Type 6 (Loyalist)

Most Common Match If the:	

Man is Type 1 (Reformer)	A woman is Type 2 (Helper)
Man is Type 2 (Helper)	A woman is Type 4 (Artist)
Man is Type 3 (Achiever)	A woman is Type 9 (Peacemaker)
Man is Type 4 (Artist)	A woman is Type 2 (Helper)
Man is Type 5 (Thinker)	A woman is Type 1 (Perfectionist)
Man is Type 6 (Loyalist)	A woman is Type 2 (Helper)
Man is Type 7 (Enthusiast)	A woman is Type 1 (Perfectionist)
Man is Type 8 (Leader)	A woman is Type 2 (Helper)
Man is Type 9 (Peacemaker)	A woman is Type 4 (Artist)

From this same study, we've learned that men and women choose their partners differently.

Type Two (Helpers) and Type Eight (Leaders) do not go together that frequently. Women Type Two (Helpers) should be listed as being also commonly found with men Type Eight (Leaders). When it comes to combined frequency, gender makes a difference.

For instance:

Male type Nine (Peacemakers) with female Type Four (Artists) are frequently seen as a ready-made match (there were 16 couples in this study). But Type Four male with Type Nine female artists are exceptionally rare.

Female Type Eight (Leaders) with male Type Nine (Peacemakers) has also been identified. But male Type Eight (Leaders) with females Type Two (Helpers) and Type Six (Loyalists) were found more frequently.

By Way of Conclusion

Dear Reader,

Alas, the journey has all but come to an end, but promises were made and you've learned a lot from what this book has to offer. The Enneagram is a tool for discovering one's inner beauty, mapping out one's understanding of the world, and learning how you relate to it and and all of humankind. It is no exaggeration to say that the study of the Enneagram cuts across all scopes and applications of human endeavor, ranging from psychology, sports, education, business, leadership, vriminal justice, parenting, etc.

Just like the words of George Ivanovitch Gurdjieff:

"I would like to show you the way to speed up your pace, But it is not the way to happiness— Happiness is the way."

The goal of the Enneagram is to give you firm control over yourself, your environment, and anything you crave. Indeed, all that people truly crave is unconditional peace and happiness in their pursuit of success. Unfortunately, the world has continuously presented nothing but pangs of evildoing and disabling conditions that prevent us from unleashing our full potential.

In providing a viable alternative to this chaos, this book covering the tenets of the Enneagram eschews a methodological outline of ways of harnessing the information leading to self-discovery and continuous and harmonious development of the vital component centers of the body (mental, physical, and emotional). In this way, readers can gain self-help without dependence on circumstantial changes of black swan scenarios

SPECIAL BONUS!

Want These 2 Bonus Books for <u>free</u>?

Get FREE, unlimited access to these and all of my new books by joining My Book Community!